AF396014

PARKLIFE

For Ed and Maya – my heart and my home.

Green spaces pictured on double-page spreads in order of sequence:

Walthamstow Marshes, Hampstead Heath, Hyde Park, River Lea,
New River Walk, Hampstead Heath, Kew Gardens.

PARKLIFE

A love letter to London's green spaces

SOPHIA SPRING

HOXTON MINI PRESS

INTRODUCTION
David Nicholls

We didn't call it the park; it was the 'rec', as in 'recreation ground'. A flat, featureless oblong of patchy grass, sodden in winter, parched in summer, scattered with ring-pulls and dog mess – this was the late 70s – its great featureless expanse broken only by buckled goalposts and a few skinny, unclimbable trees. I hated the rec, partly because of the threat of team sports, partly because of the possibility of violence – the two seemed to go together – but during those long, endless days of summer, when the glare of sunlight on the TV screen became too much, we were harried out of the house to 'get some fresh air'. And so we loitered on that great barren prairie, an immense waiting room, wondering why anyone would go to the park out of choice.

Last summer, there were queues at the gates of Clissold Park and anyone wanting to exercise in Highbury Fields was advised to go early to avoid the rush hour. All over the city, the parks began to resemble the sites of the festivals that had all been cancelled and if Londoners had ever taken their green spaces for granted, there was no danger of that now. In the space of six months, they'd been repurposed as meeting rooms, nightclubs, concert halls, theatres and cinemas, cafés and restaurants, impromptu markets, family living rooms, gyms. London is supposedly a city of 3,000 parks and while I'm a little sceptical of that number, it's true that the city had never seemed greener than that summer. On early morning bike rides I discovered Bushy and Ruskin and Trent, Peckham Rye and Beckenham Place and Ladywell Fields. I discovered the canals and waterways that link them too, the bloodstream of London, captured so brilliantly by Sophia in these photographs. Walk north on the Lea, west or east on the Grand Union, south on the Wandle or the Waterlink Way and you can see the ghosts of London's old industries, cranes and disused warehouses and old pumping stations. Keep walking for the rest of the day, under the pylons and past the depots, and you can feel the city fading behind you, the skies opening up.

The photographs in this volume are a fine portrait of that strange time,
the diversity of people and place and the sense of community too. It's good
to see the less familiar urban parks feature so prominently: Burgess, Springfield,
Mile End, places that don't pretend to be countryside. The Royal Parks are
beautiful and elegant, but they feel as if they belong to someone else (which of
course they do) and if these photos show anything, it's that our essential green
spaces are shaped by the communities who live around them and use them every
day. There's youth and noise and fun here and music played too loud, but
also that particular melancholy, the half-pleasurable sadness of a cloudy day
at the end of summer with the days shortening, the leaves beginning to curl.

But for the most part, this is a portrait of a city that relishes its public play-
grounds and which now, as I write, is stepping outside again after a long winter,
revisiting friends and family, eating, drinking, flirting, celebrating, a city that
is at its liveliest not on its streets but in its scuffed, scrappy, beautiful green spaces.

May 2021

PHOTOGRAPHER'S NOTE
Sophia Spring

In the spring of 2020 I found myself, like many, knocked sideways. The world became untethered – all our rituals of normality removed against the backdrop of a global pandemic. But then something magical happened: the first buds of spring appeared, and the bright April sunshine beckoned us outside. We ventured to our local parks for our single dose of daily exercise and, perhaps for the first time, we noticed the crocuses appear and the slow blossoming of the trees. Without the steady hum of traffic and the airplanes in the sky, the birdsong became our new soundtrack. We were restored and calmed by the natural world on our doorsteps.

During this time my love of London's parks deepened. I've always been captivated by the life reflected in them – an almost utopian microcosm of our wider society. In a world increasingly motivated by profit and status, the park is a space that symbolises democracy. 40 percent of London's surface area is made up of publicly accessible green spaces – from parks to commons, greens, cemeteries, woodlands, waterways and marshes. These enclaves occupy some of the most expensive real estate in the world (and with some of the most breathtaking views) yet remain free and communal spaces for all – making London a unique capital city.

Last spring, I decided to pick up my camera to capture the diversity of people whose lives are enriched by these extraordinary green spaces. It is my hope that these images will transcend the time in which they were made. For while these spaces have been a lifeline for capital dwellers during lockdown, their importance precedes this time and will extend beyond it. Parks touch the lives of all Londoners – from family gatherings to first dates, walks with friends to solo rambles – and for this they should be celebrated.

In short, *Parklife* is my love letter to London's green spaces.

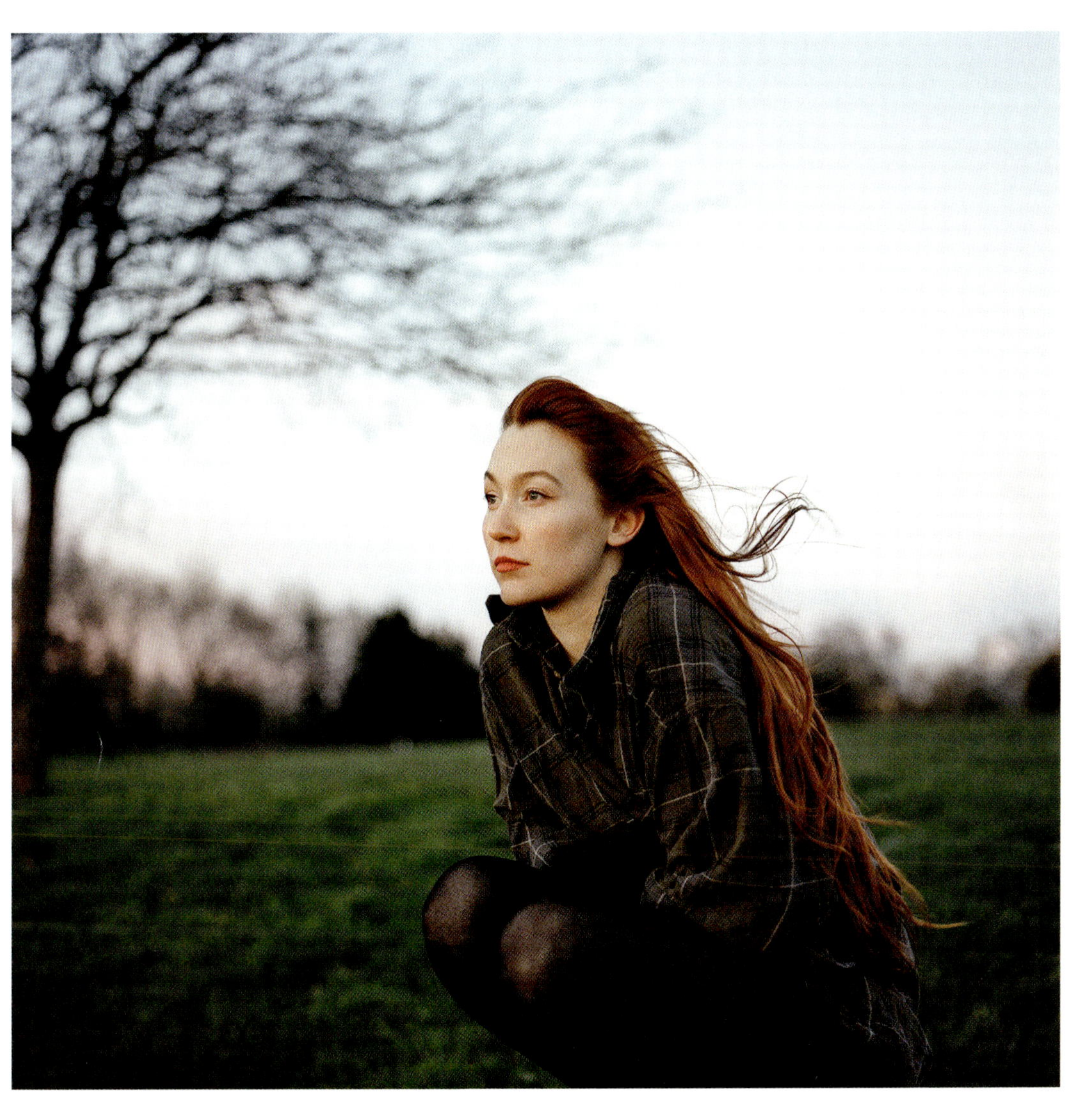

Freya

FINSBURY PARK

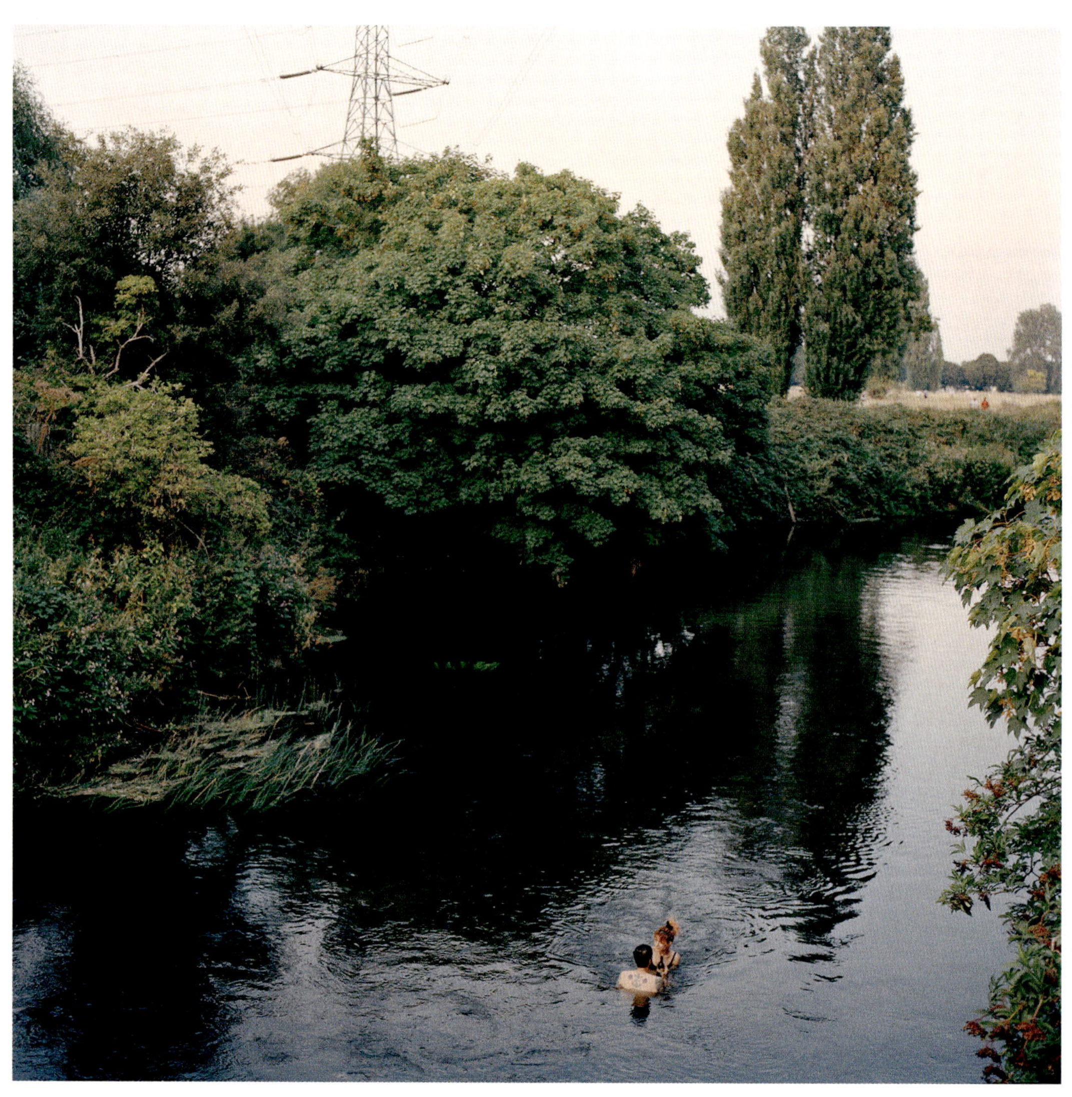

RIVER LEA

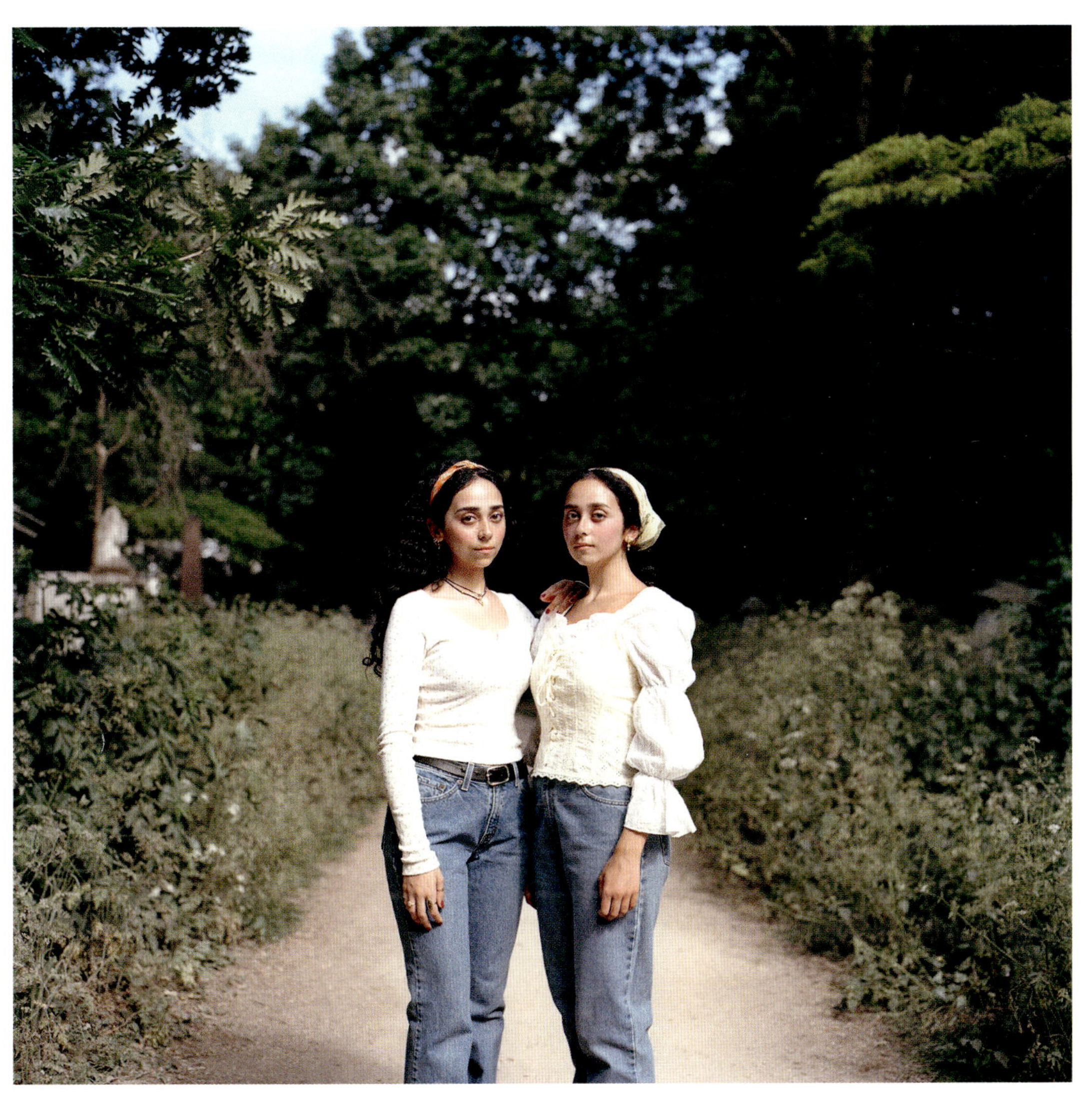

Sumayah & Sarah

ABNEY PARK

'Until recently, I didn't know the full size of Brockwell Park.
It's only through going stir-crazy indoors that I've ventured further
and explored spaces I never knew existed.'

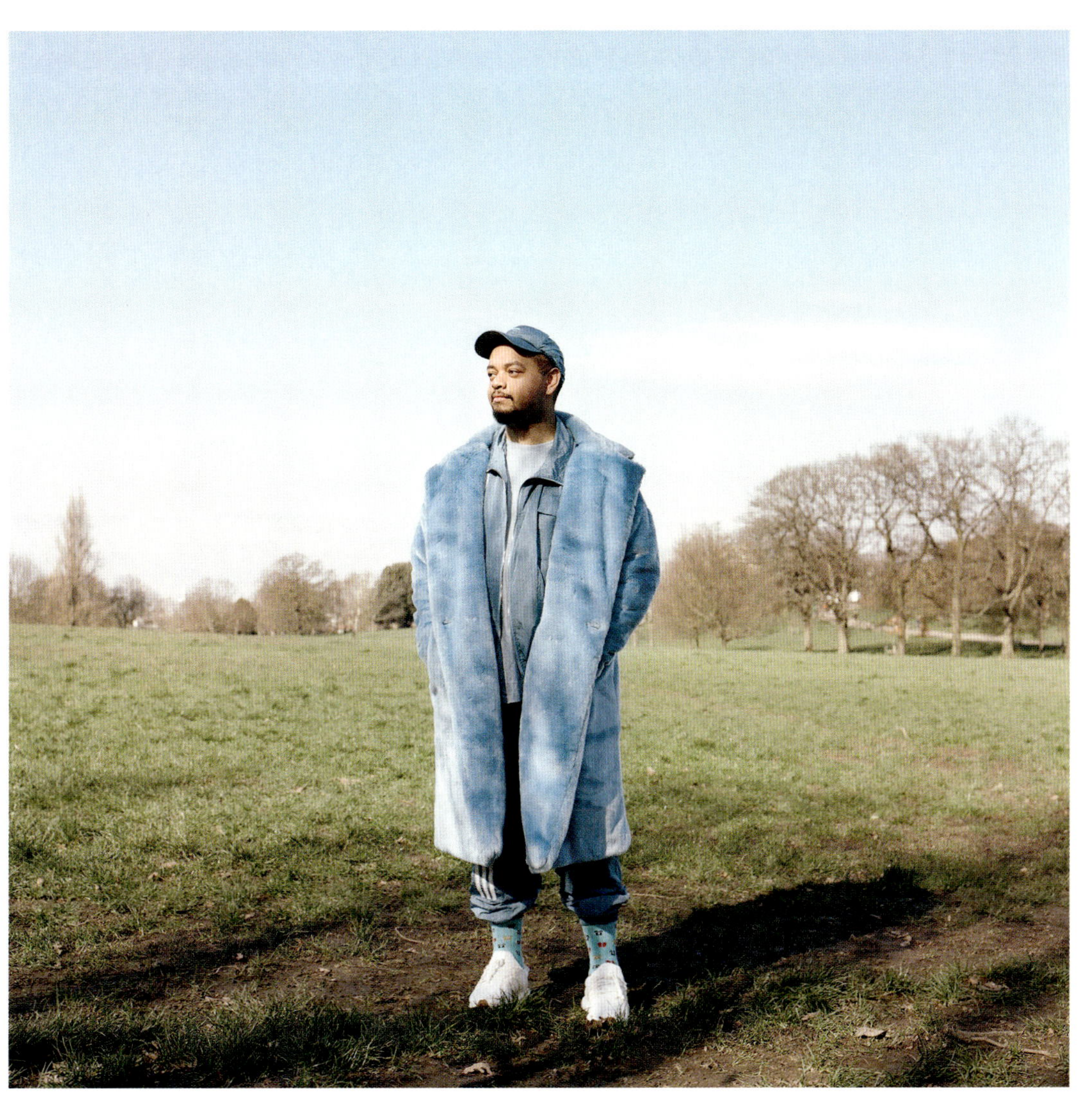

Myles

BROCKWELL PARK

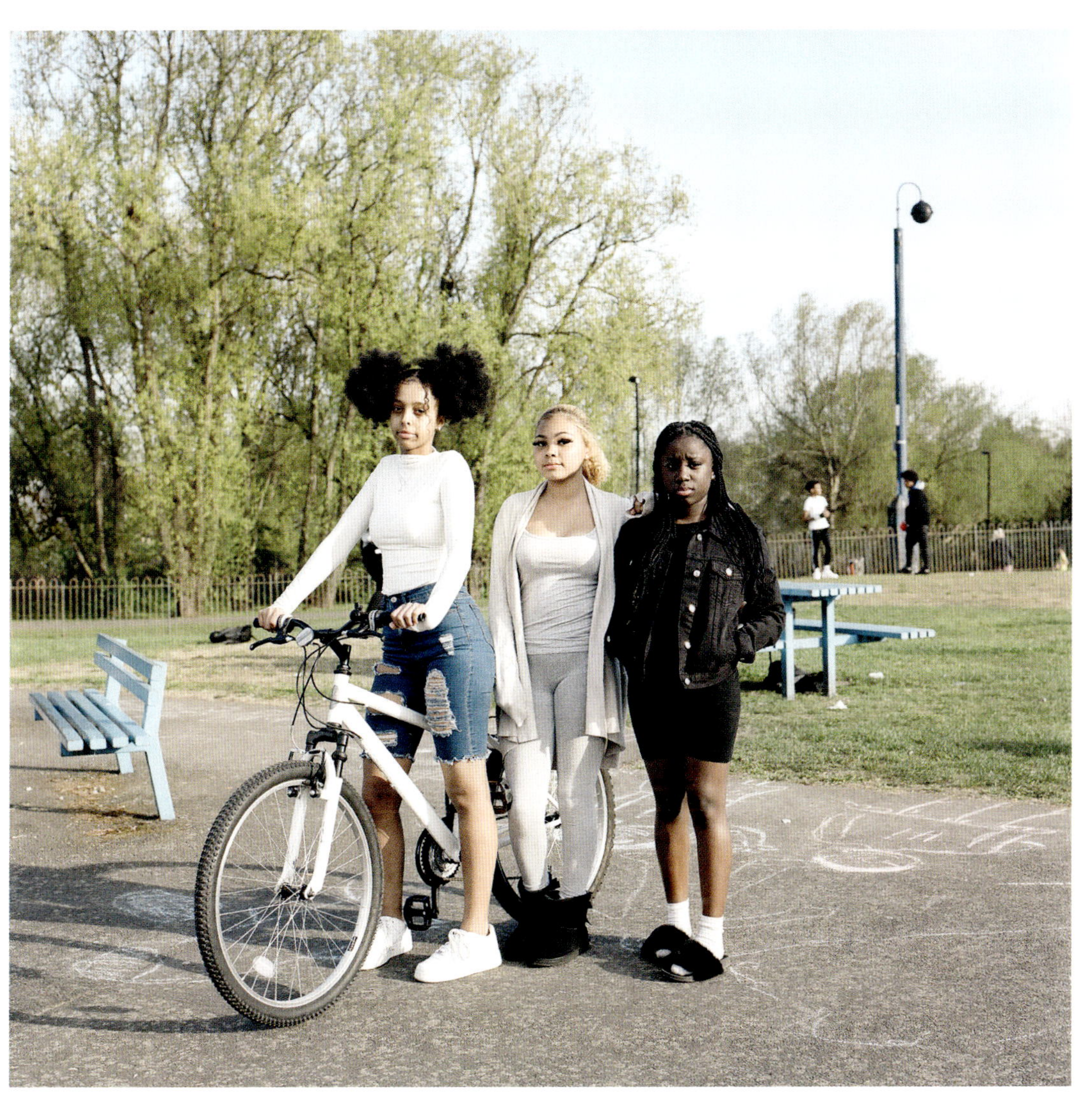

Ade, Renae & Eluya

BELLINGHAM GREEN

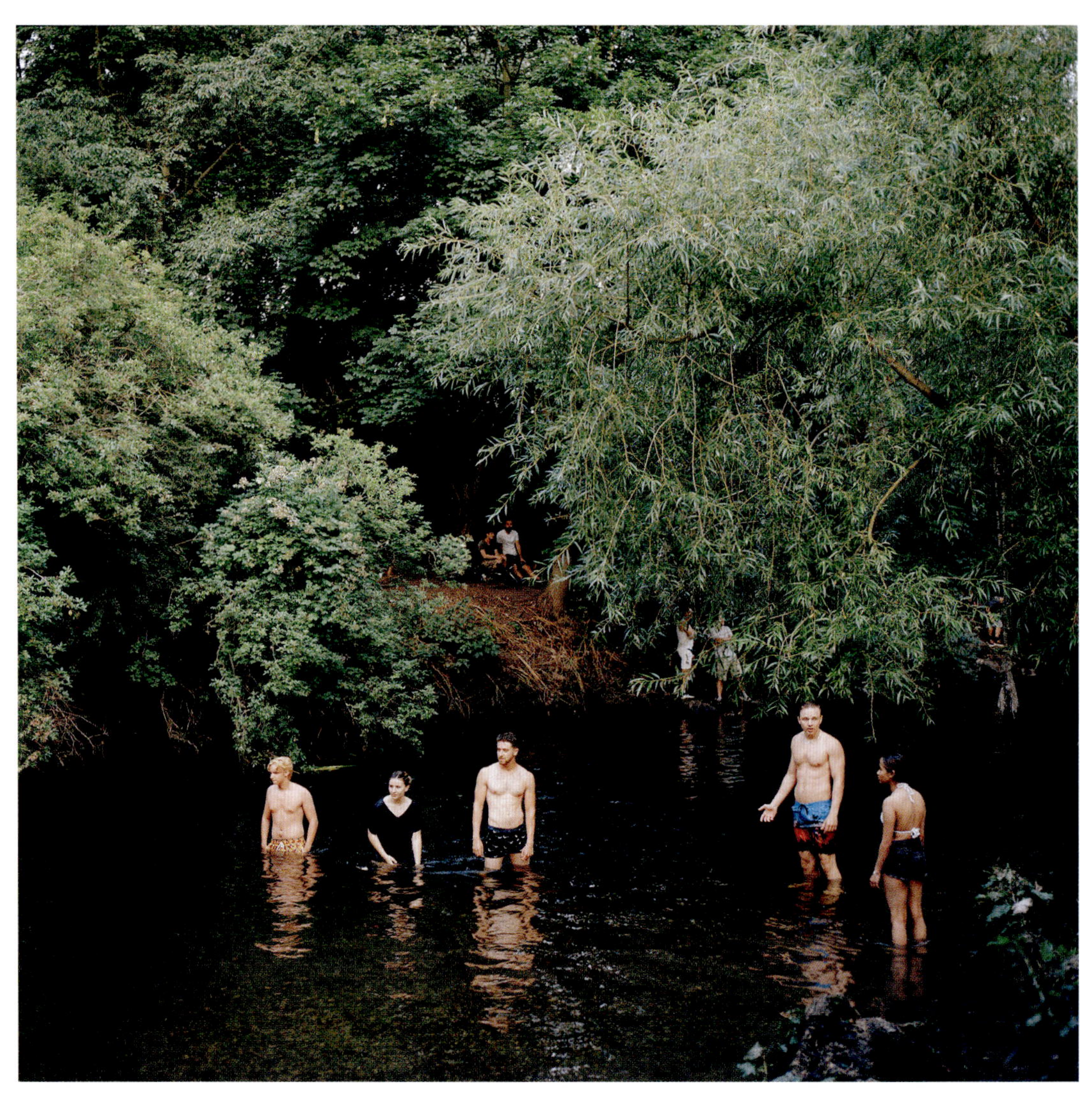

RIVER LEA

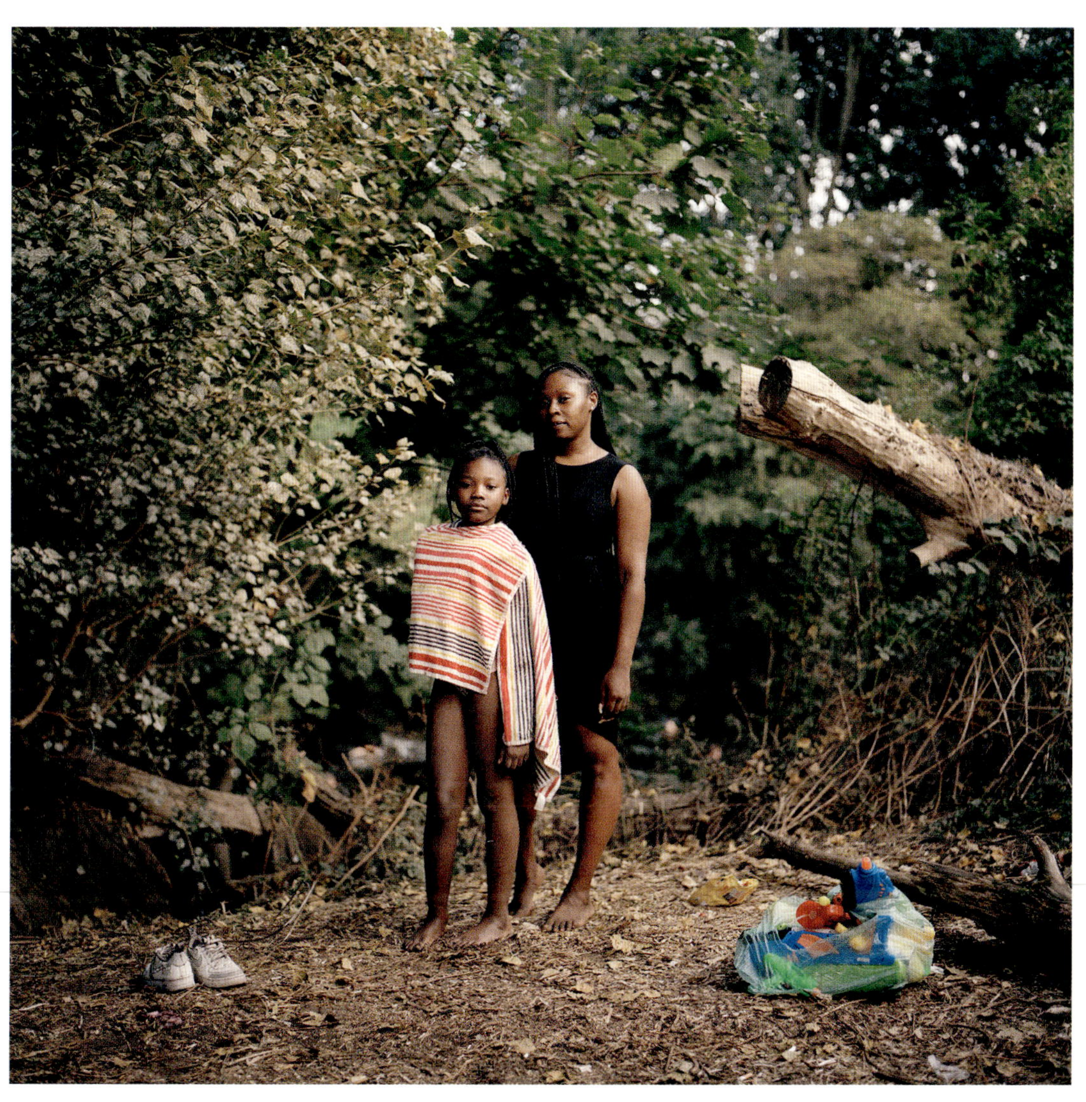

Danielle & Iyanna

HACKNEY MARSHES

'Looking back, some of our most defining moments of last year
took place in Regent's Park. We had a picnic here in summer,
on the cusp of a new lockdown. Today it feels like we've come full
circle – emerging from a dull winter, heralding the first day
of sunshine and new beginnings.'

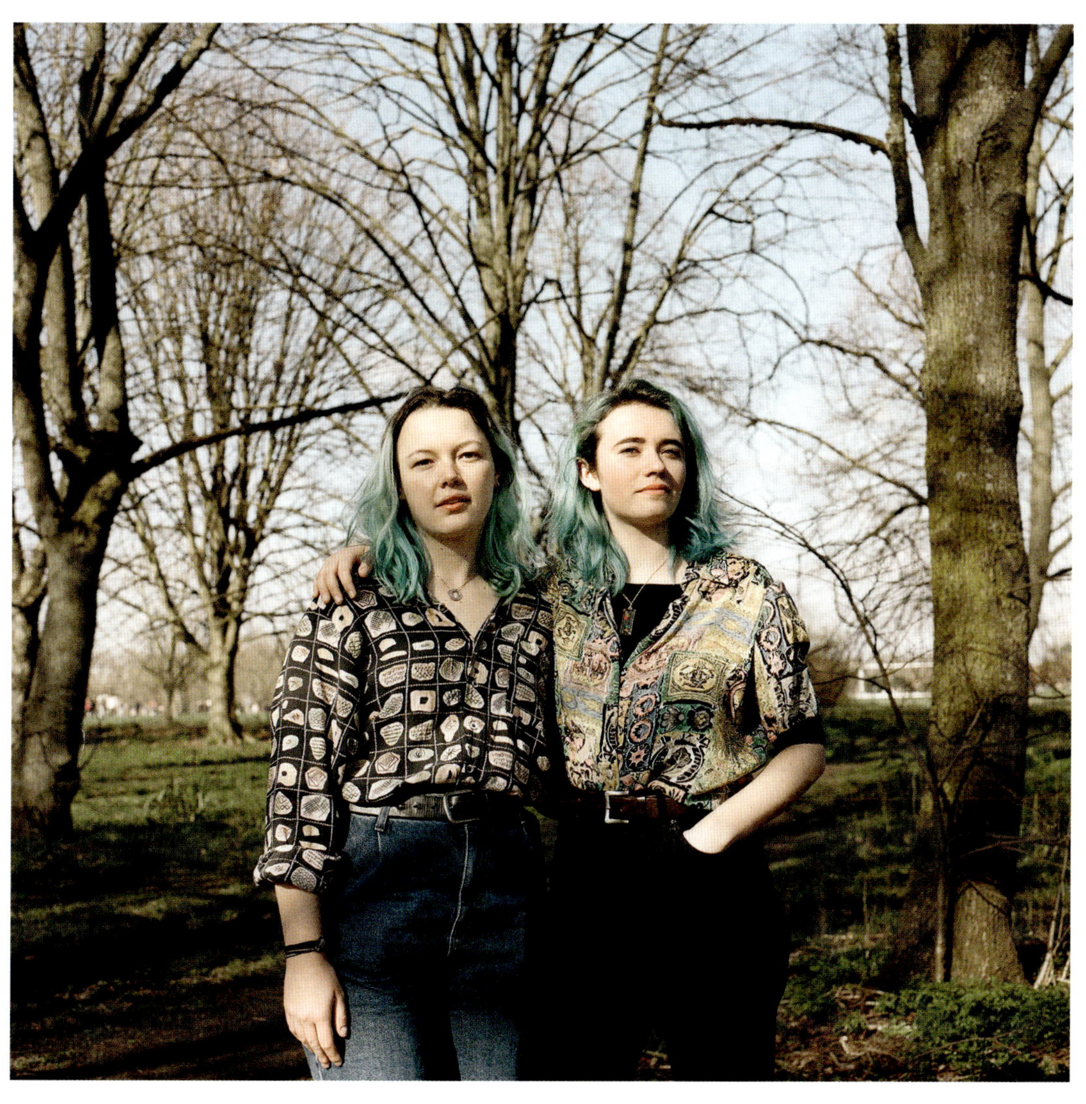

Isabella & Emma

REGENT'S PARK

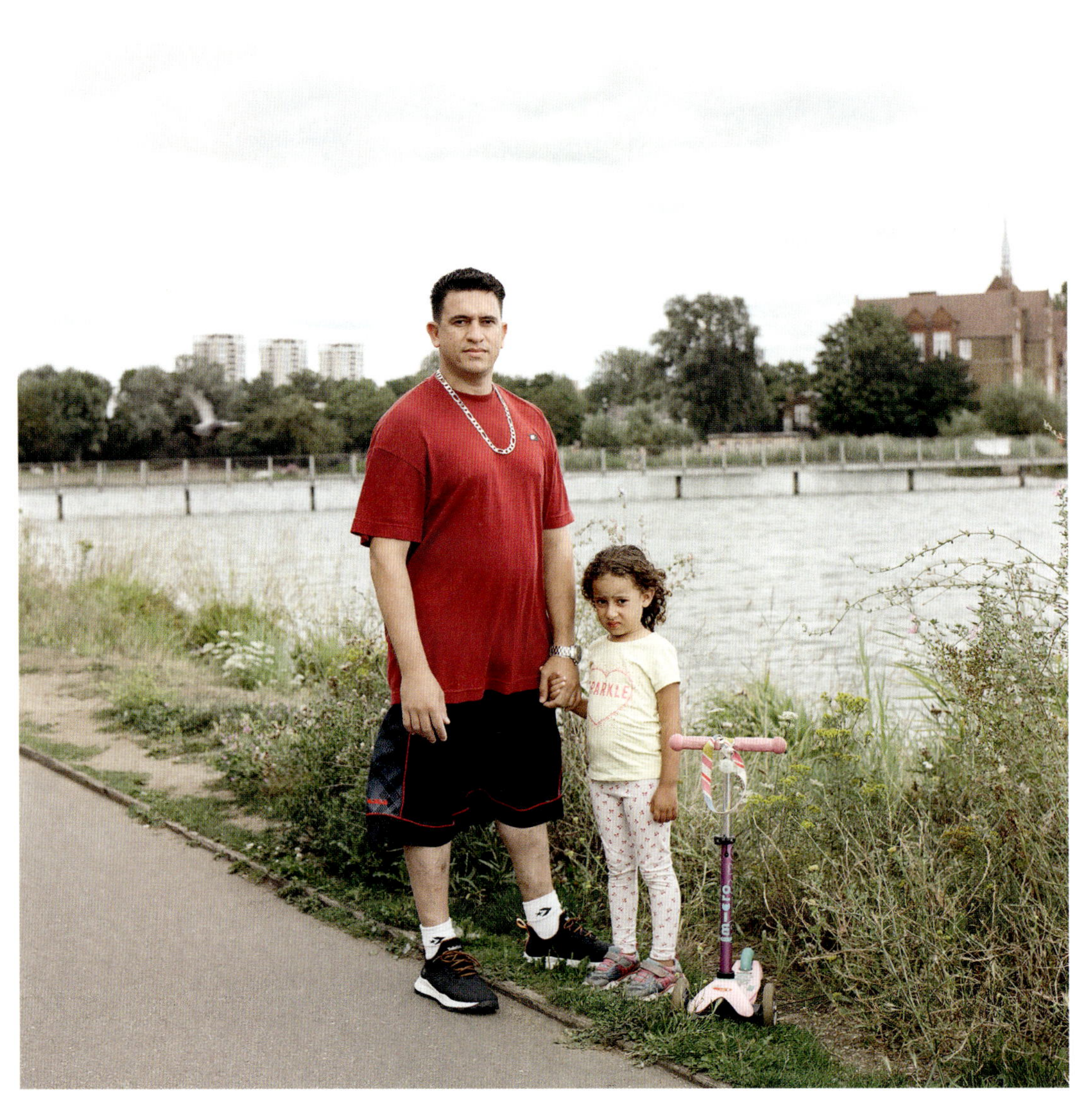

Murilo & Sophia

BURGESS PARK

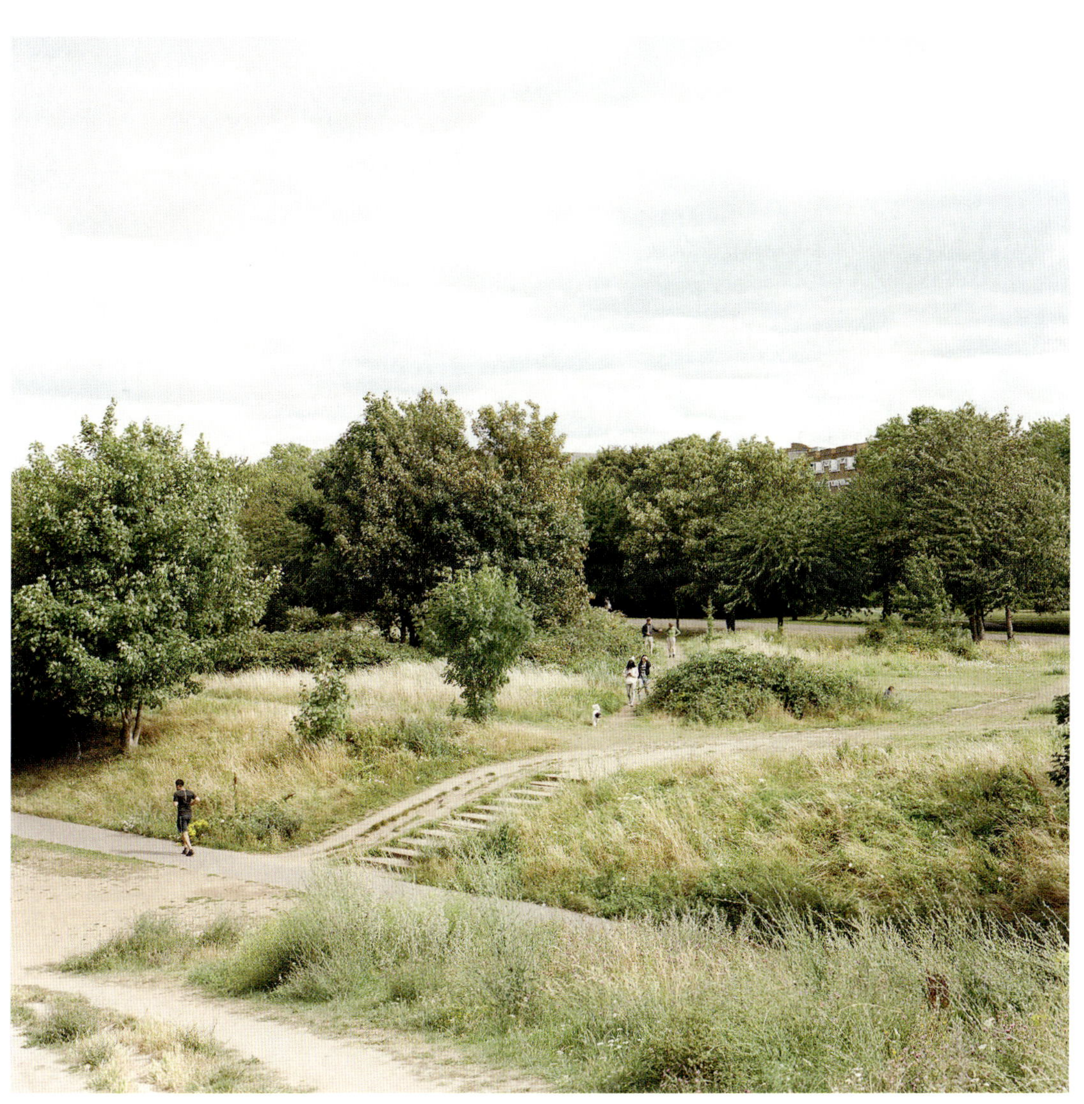

BURGESS PARK

'We come here every week; it's our special place to hang out together. It feels really peaceful being near the water. Very different from the rest of Tottenham.'

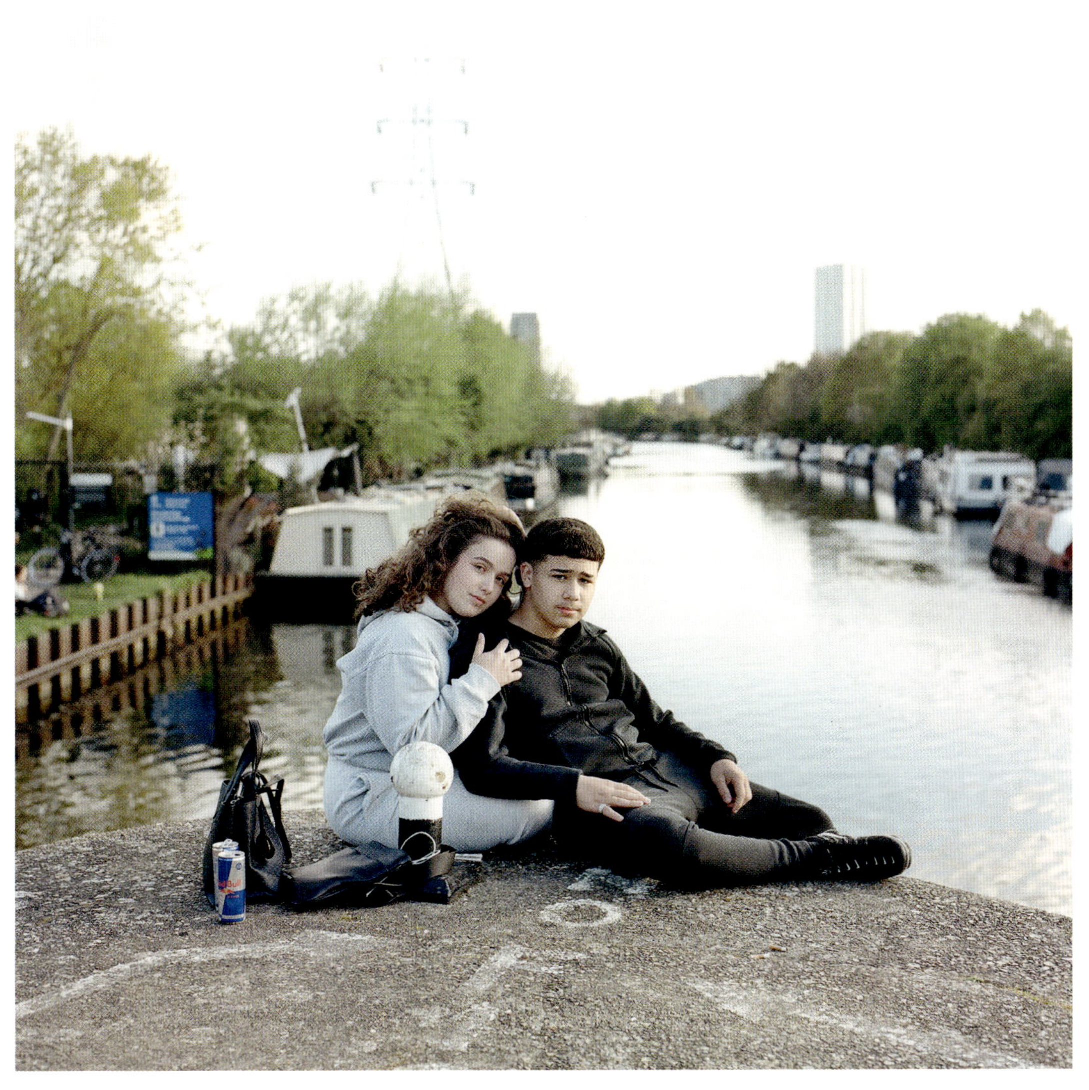

Aisa & Ahmed

TOTTENHAM MARSHES

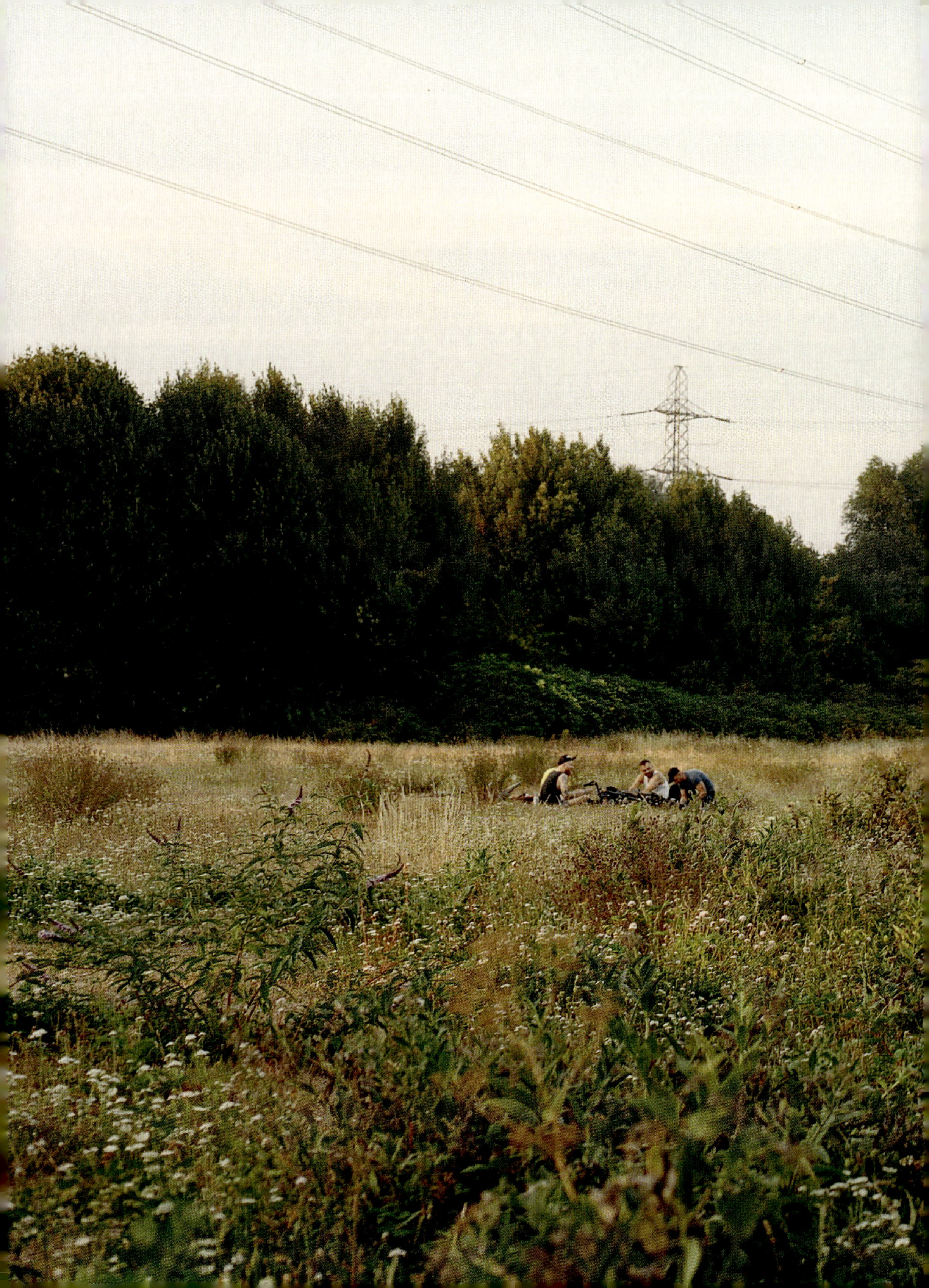

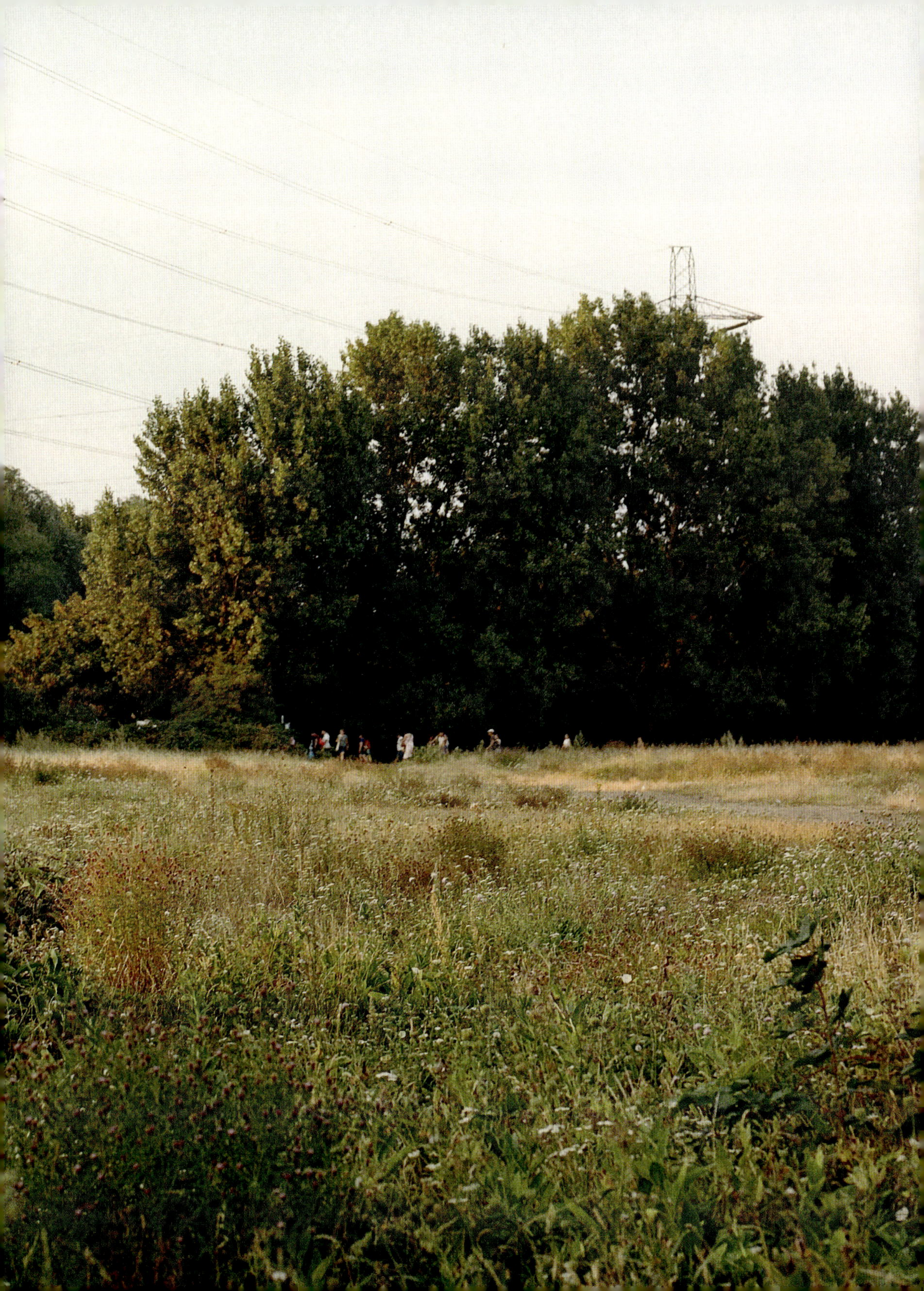

'I have been coming to Parliament Hill since I first moved to
London. Often with friends but also alone – for moments of quiet
in an occasionally overwhelming city. I'm sure I always will.'

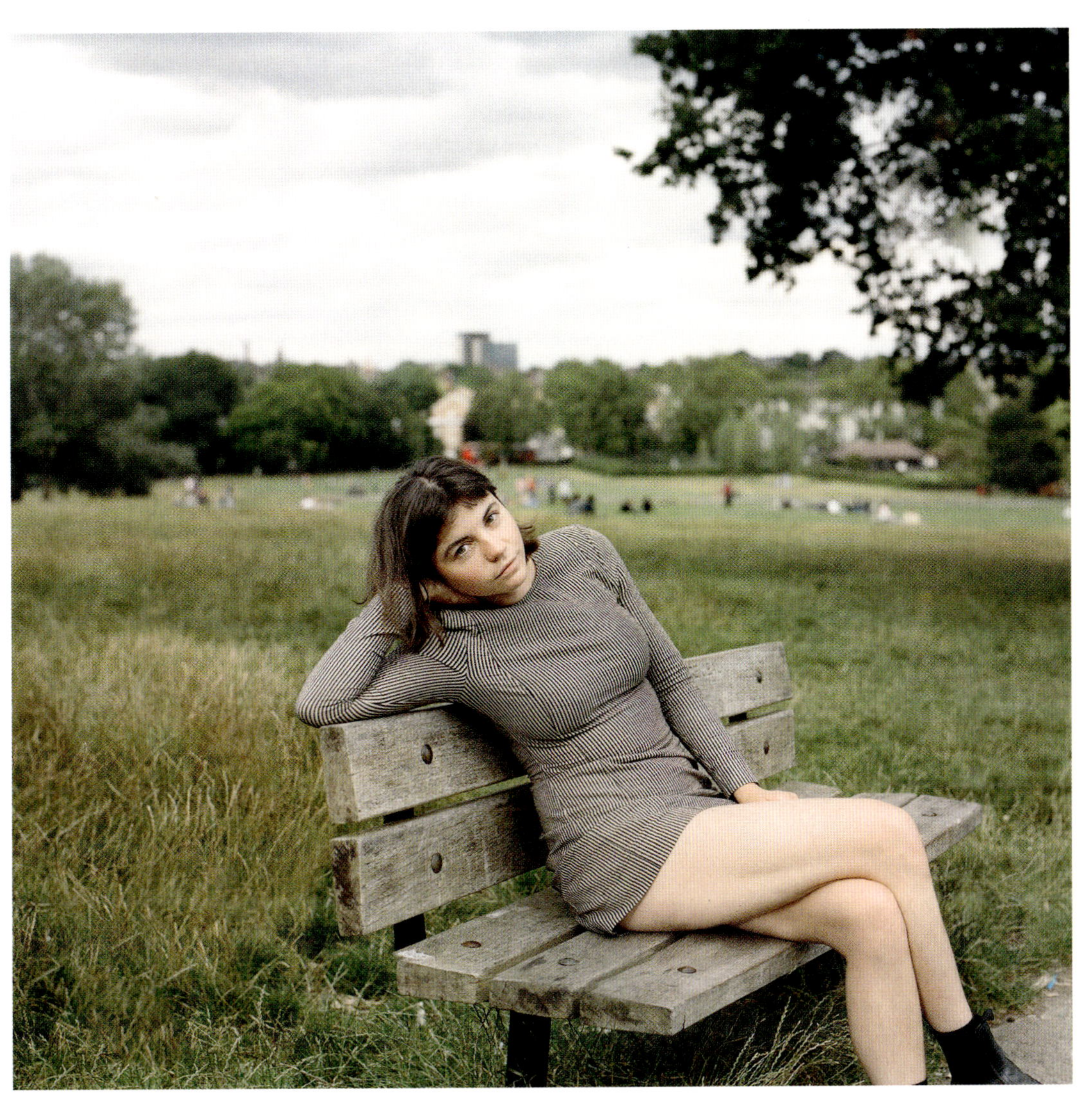

Caitlin

PARLIAMENT HILL

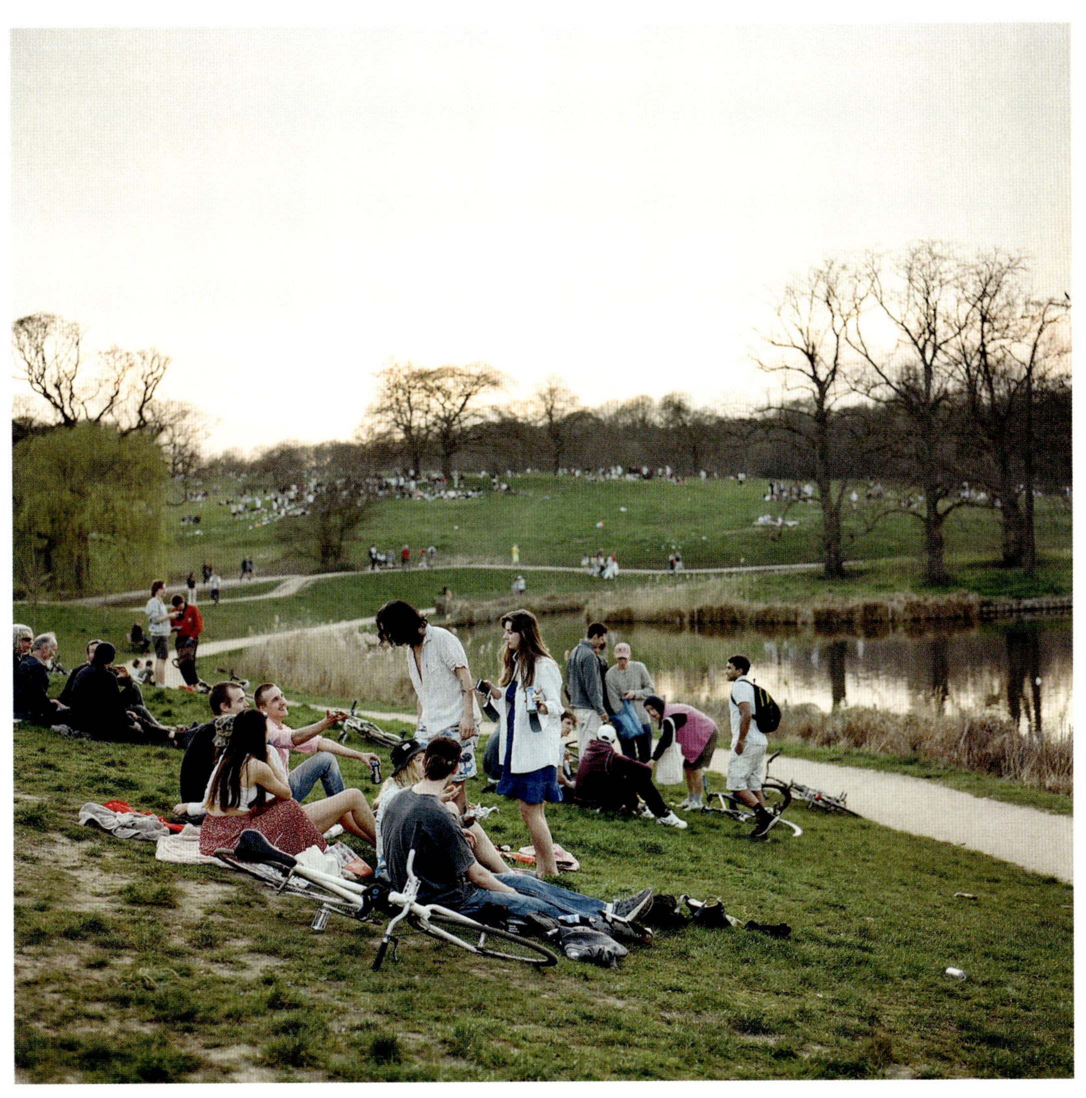

HAMPSTEAD HEATH

'London parks shaped my childhood and teen years.
Every weekend we would go to the park, sometimes ten of us and
sometimes there would be like 100. I remember when the house
party ended, we would always go to the park.'

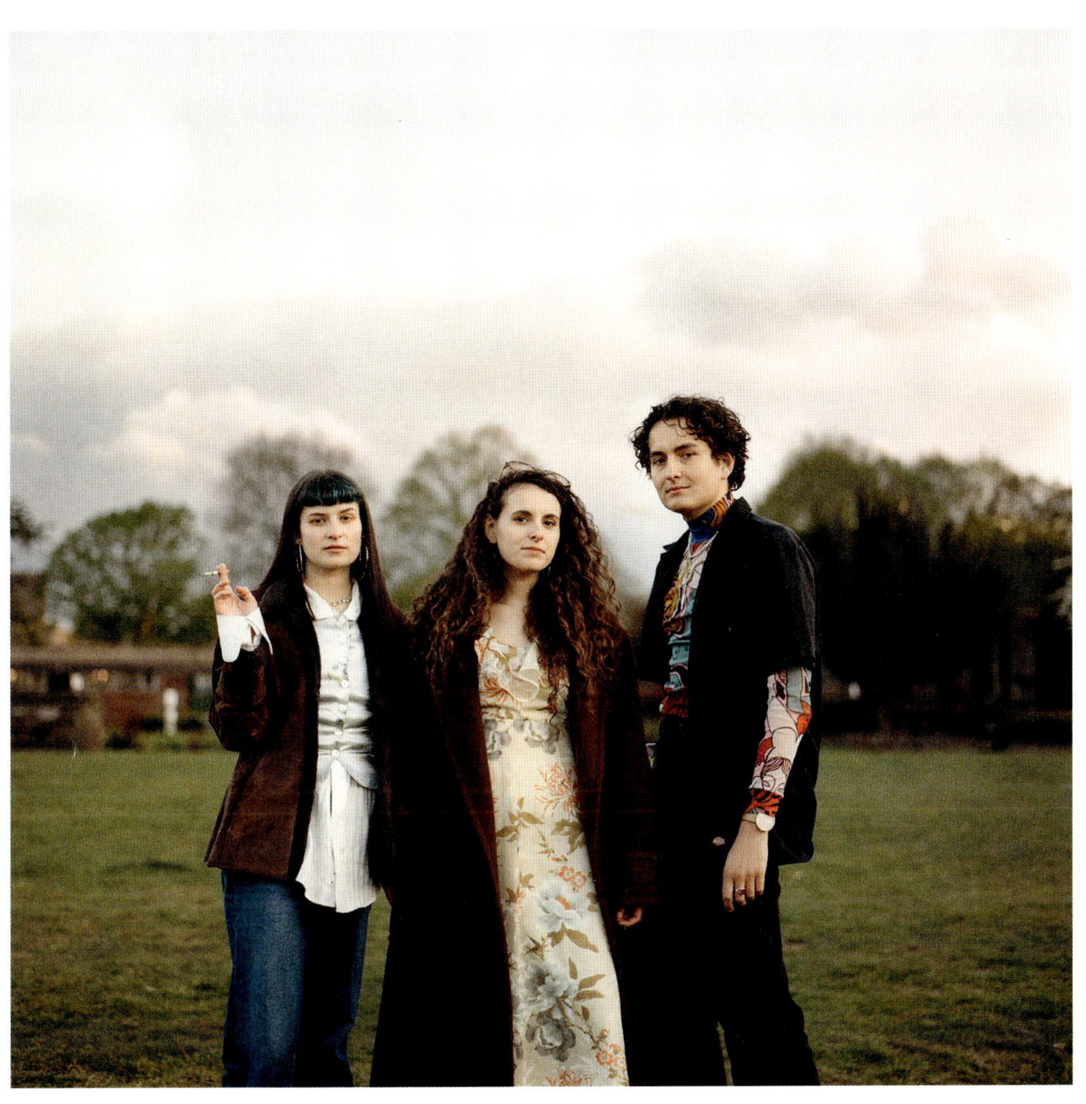

Jenny, Lyra & Ellis

HAGGERSTON PARK

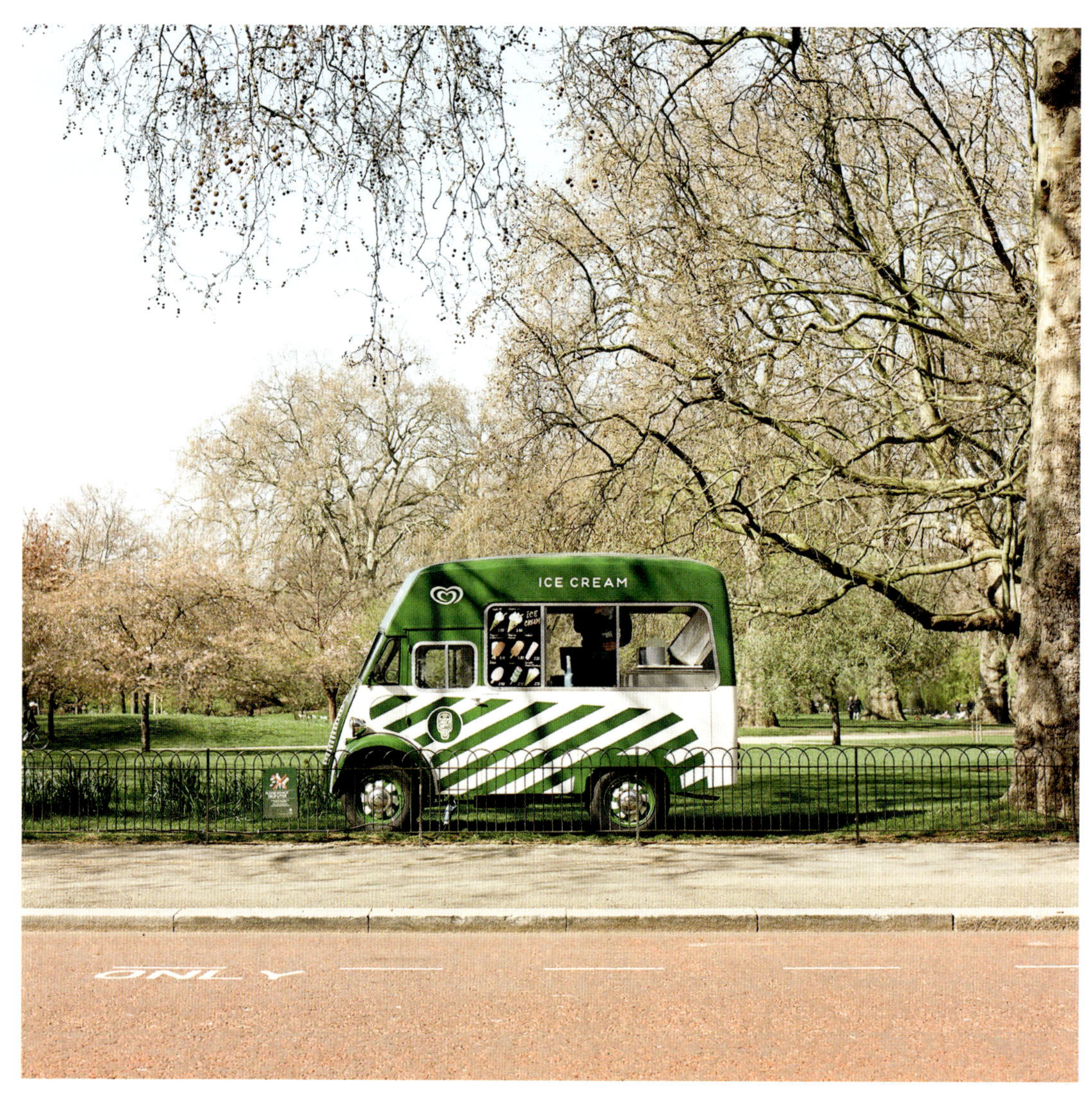

GREEN PARK

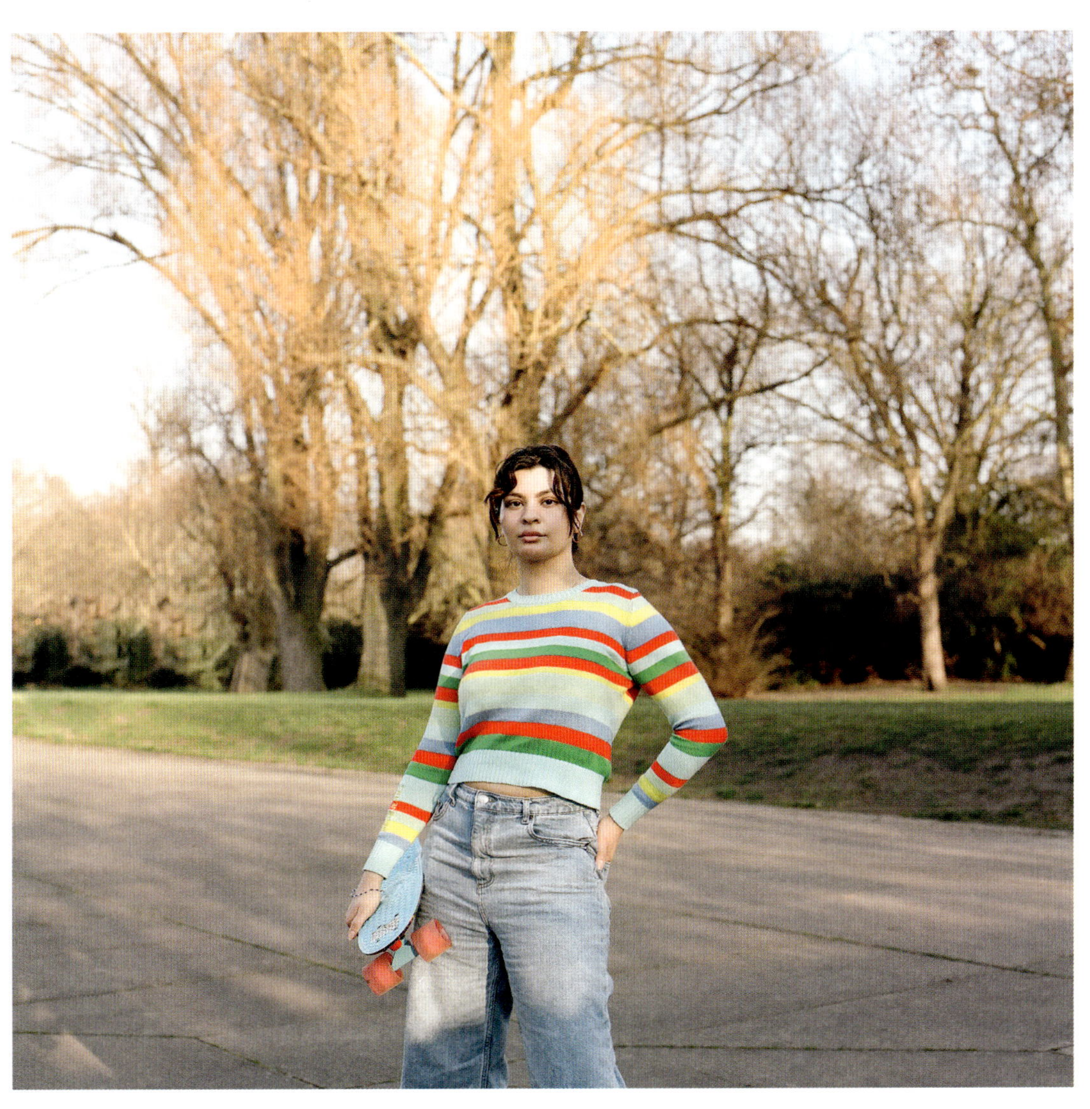

Sandy

BATTERSEA PARK

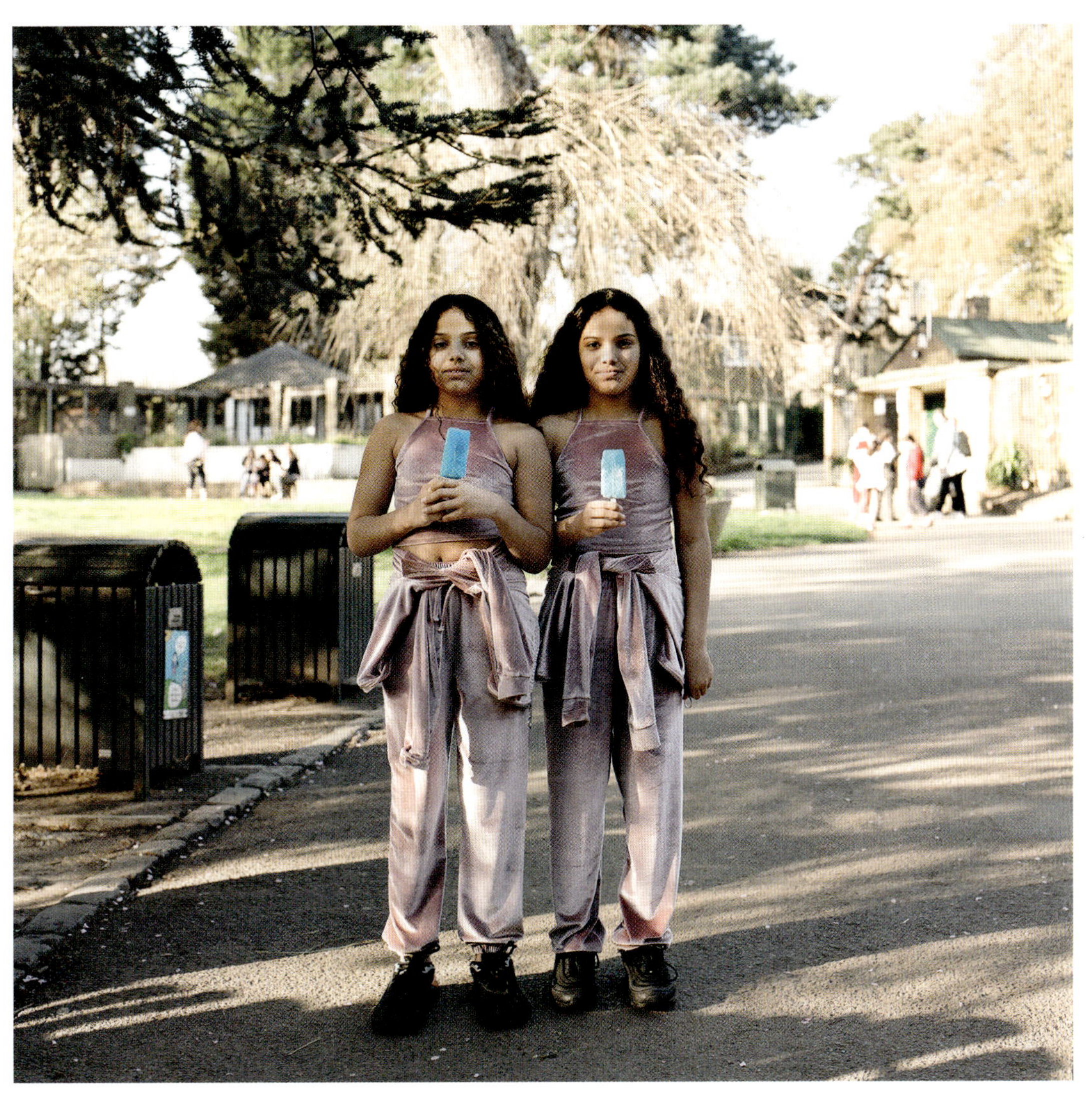

Savannah & Surayah

BUNNY PARK

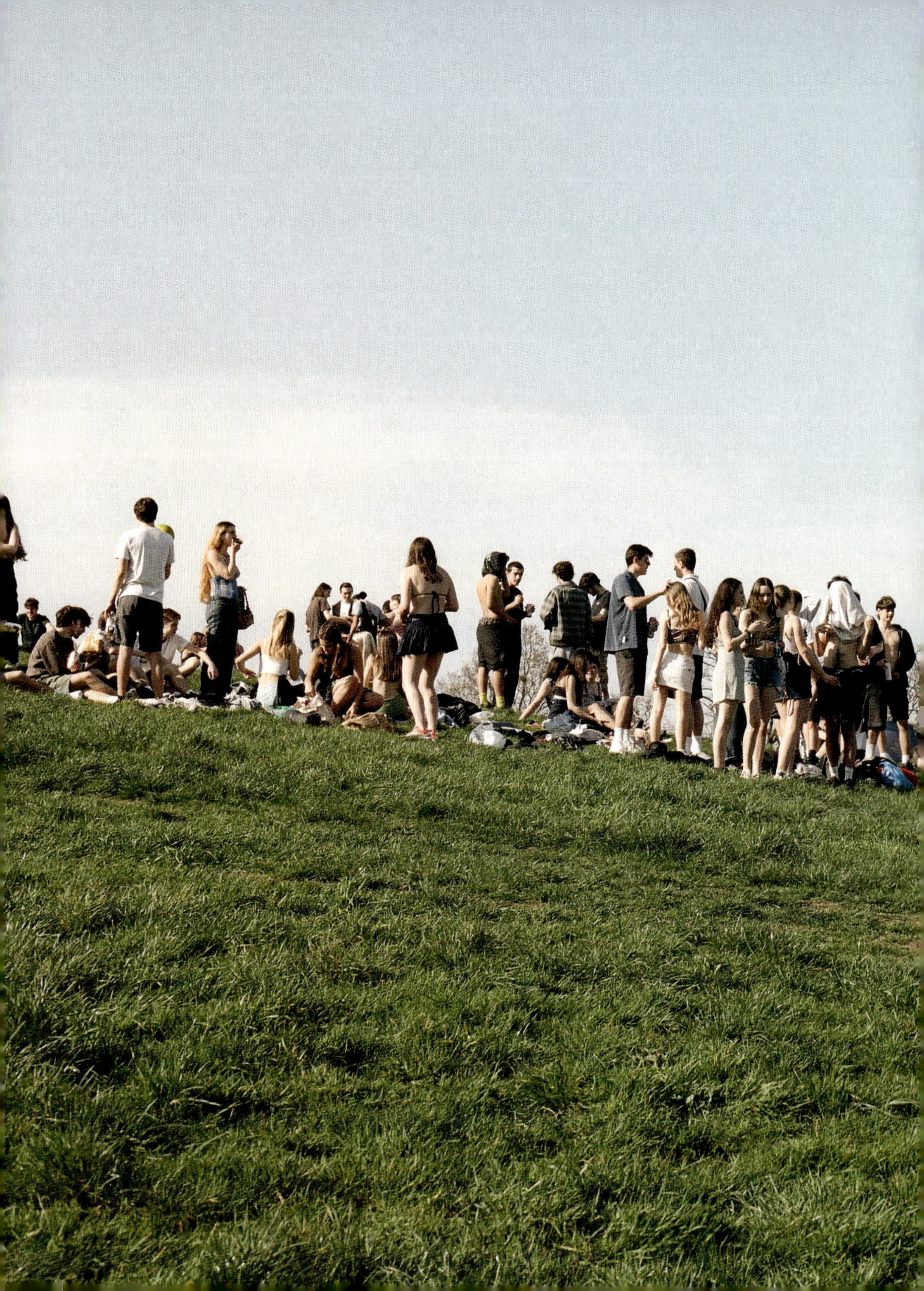

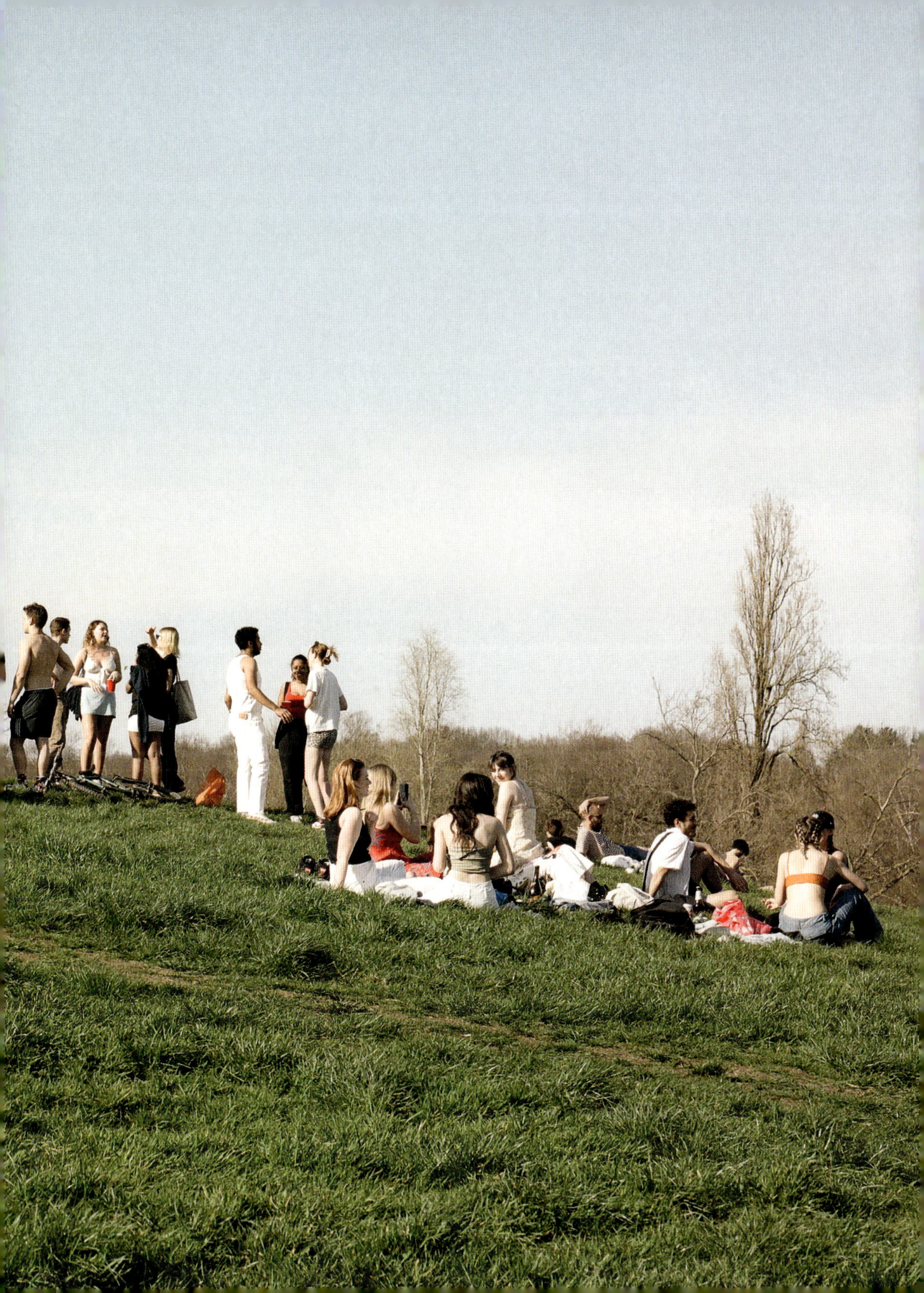

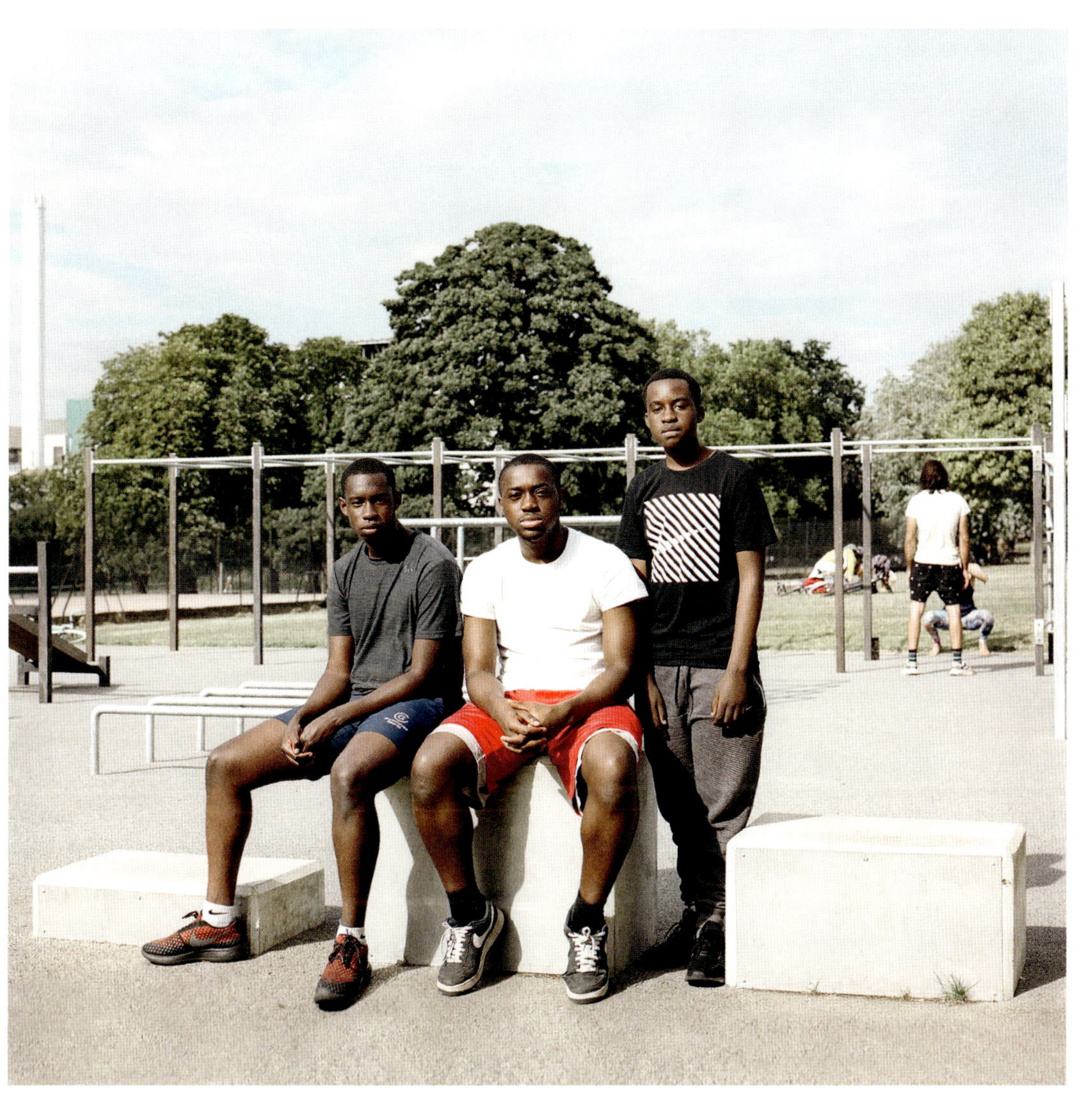

Paul, Daniel & Isaiah

RUSKIN PARK

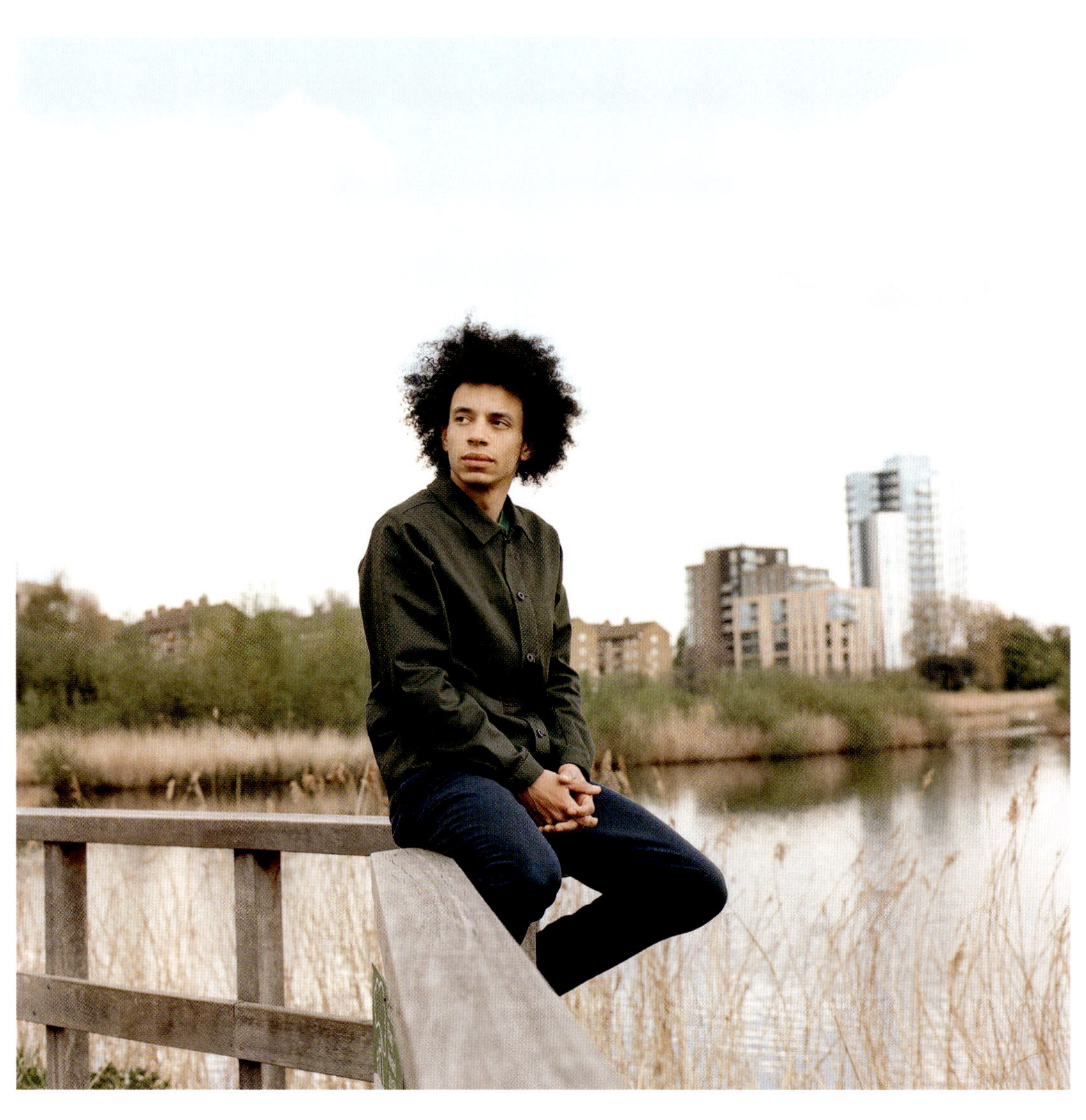

Gabriel

WOODBERRY WETLANDS

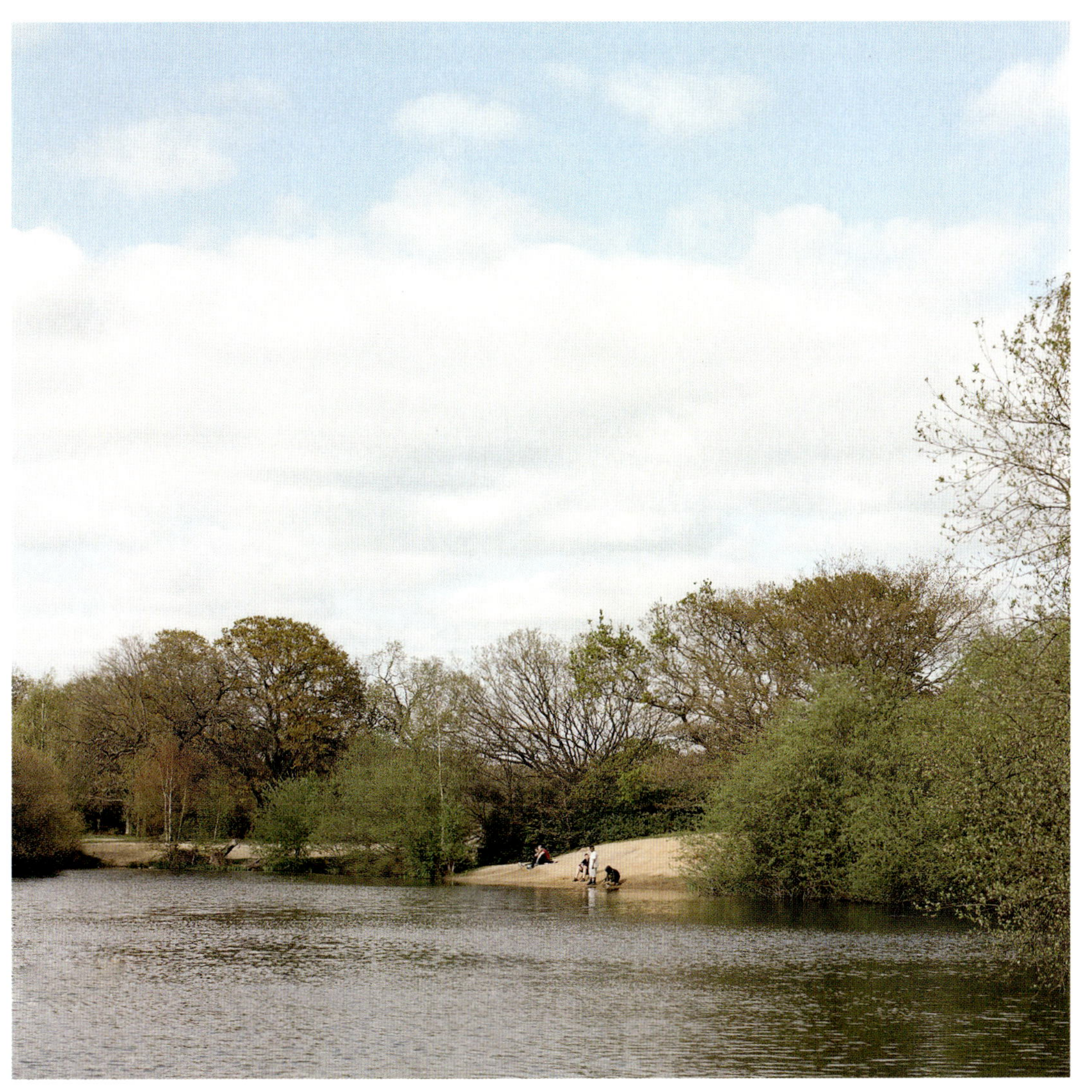

HOLLOW PONDS

'We've ridden here all the way from St Paul's Cathedral.
We're just taking a break to enjoy the view and catch our breath.'

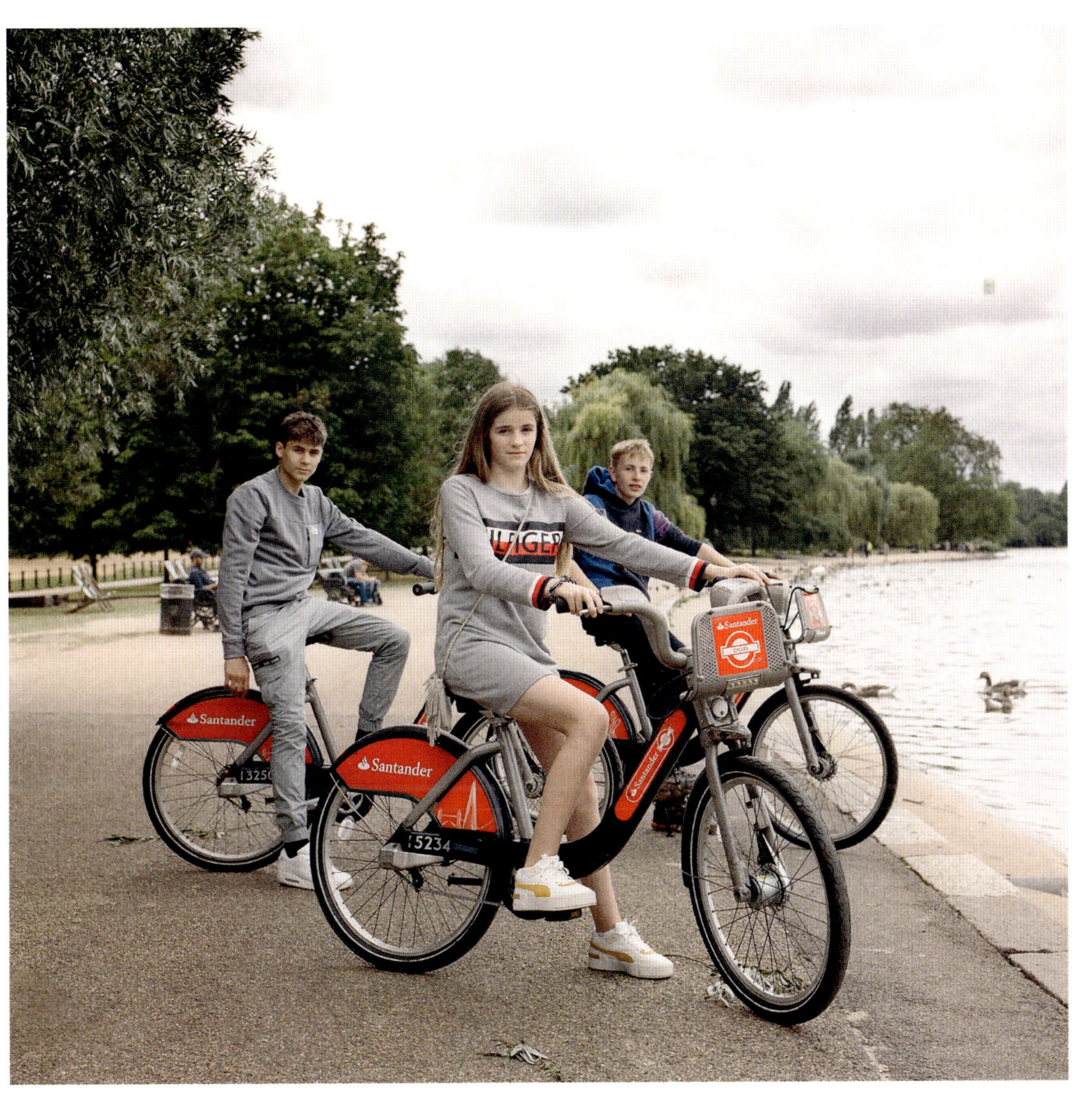

Julian, Tilly & Oscar

HYDE PARK

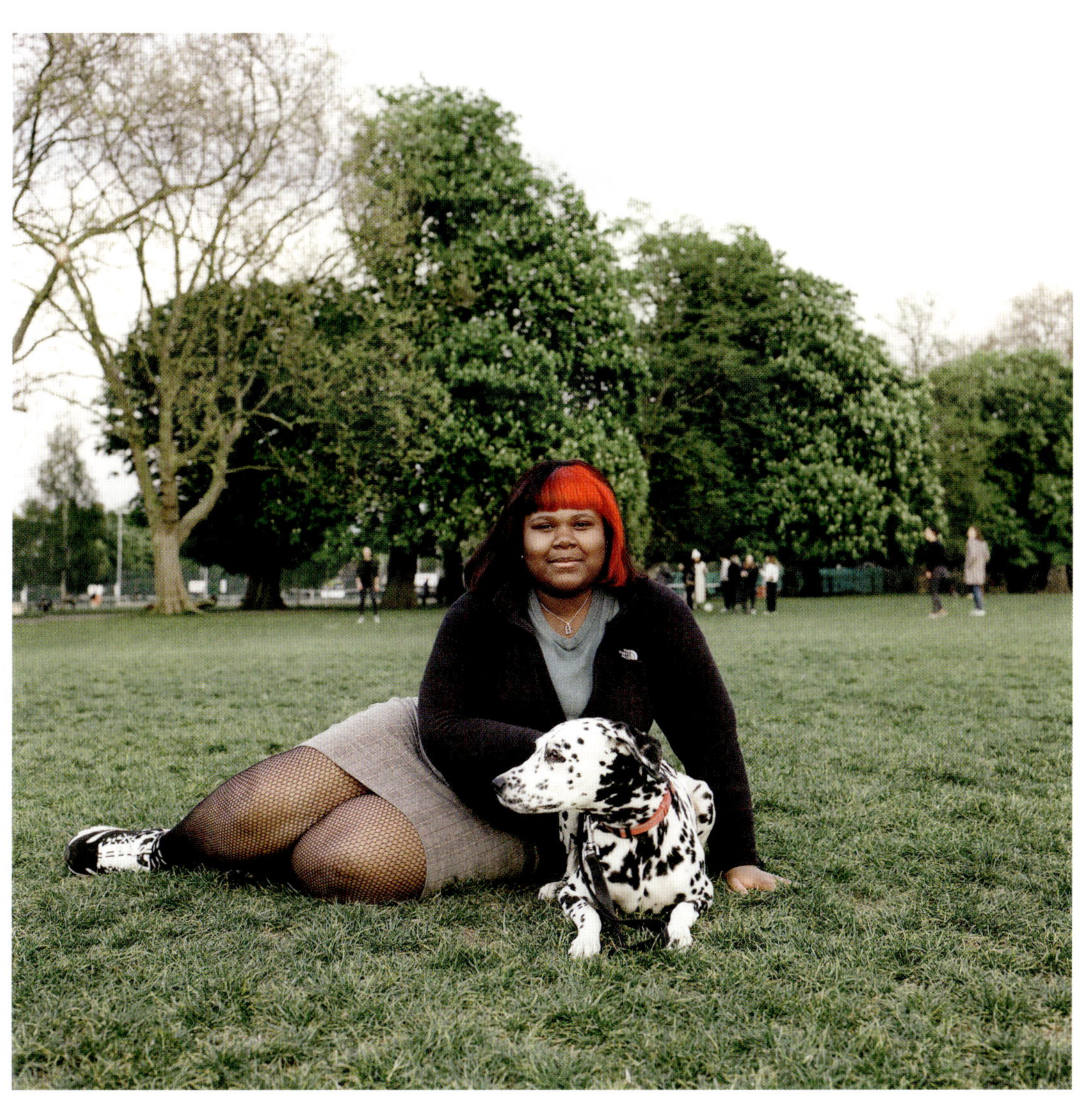

Beulah & Noa

CLISSOLD PARK

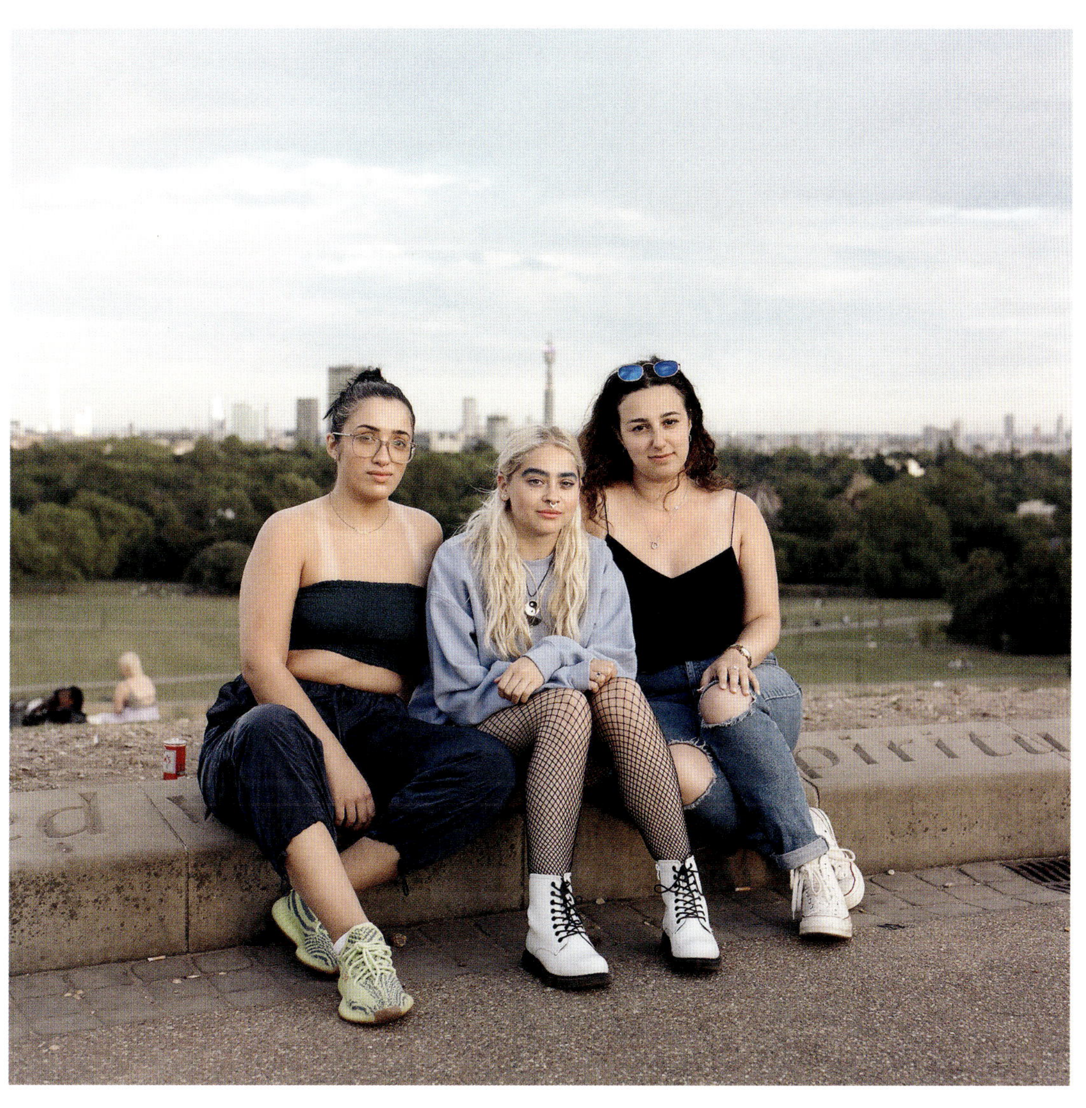

Sophie, Phoebe & Georgia

PRIMROSE HILL

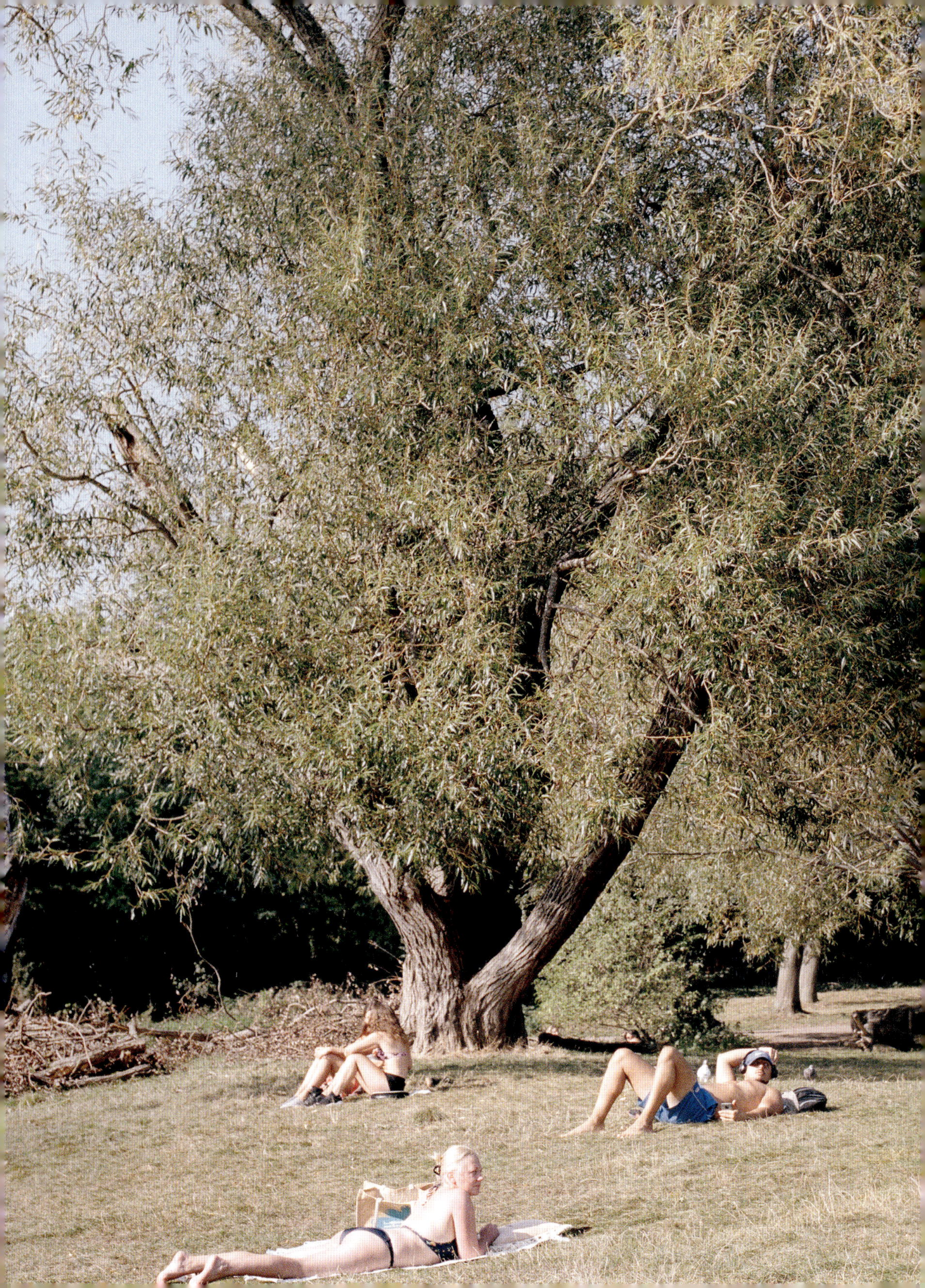

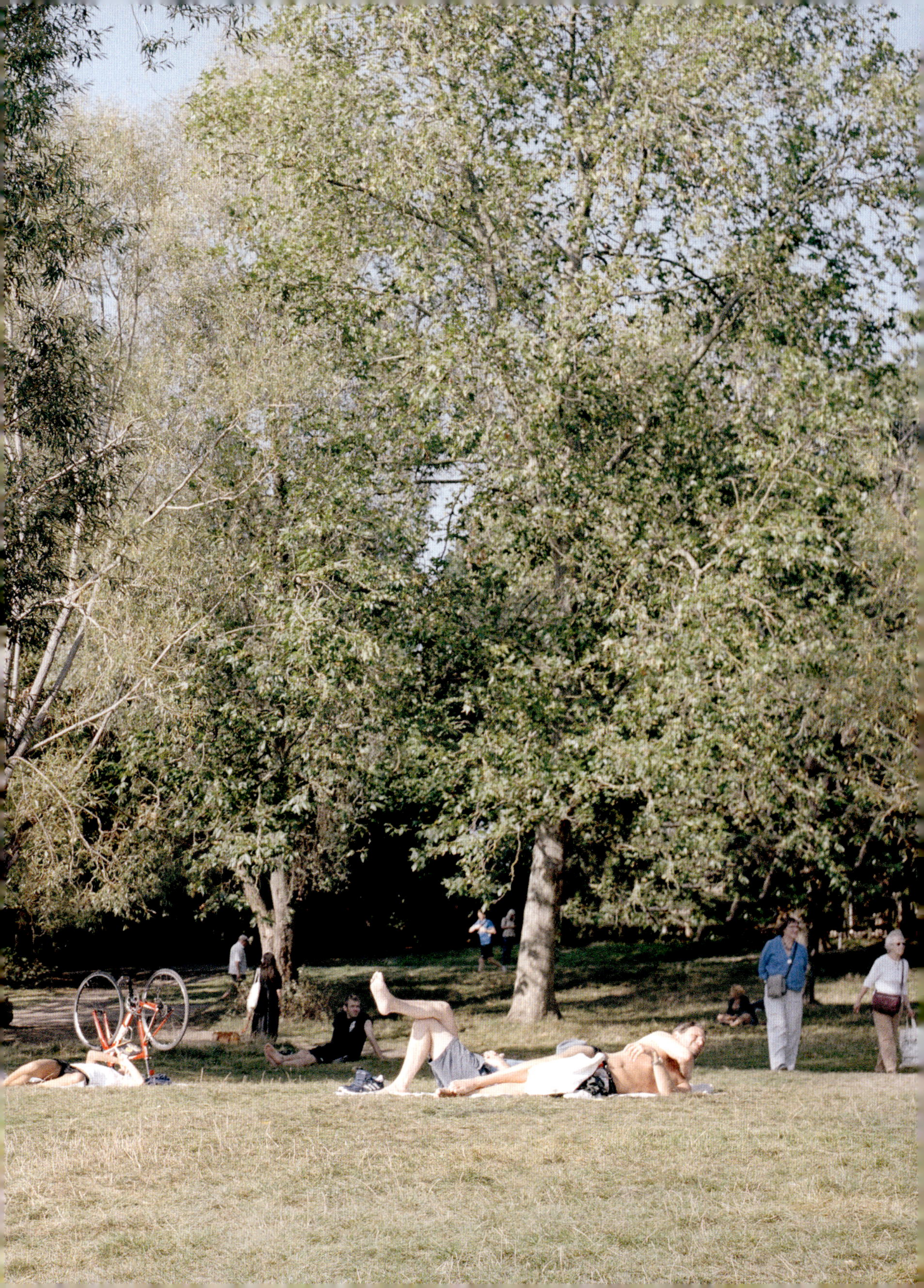

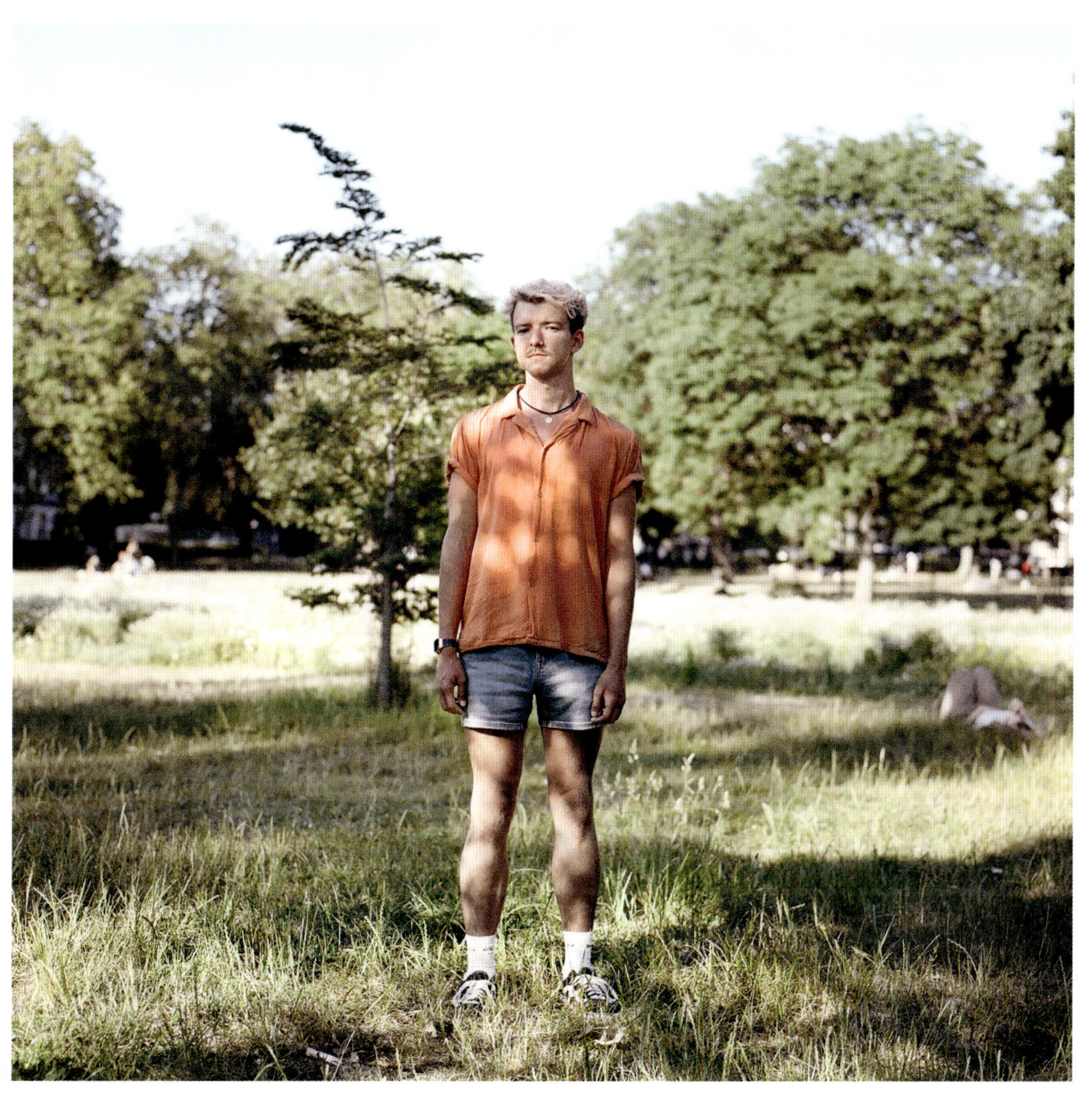

Ben

HACKNEY DOWNS

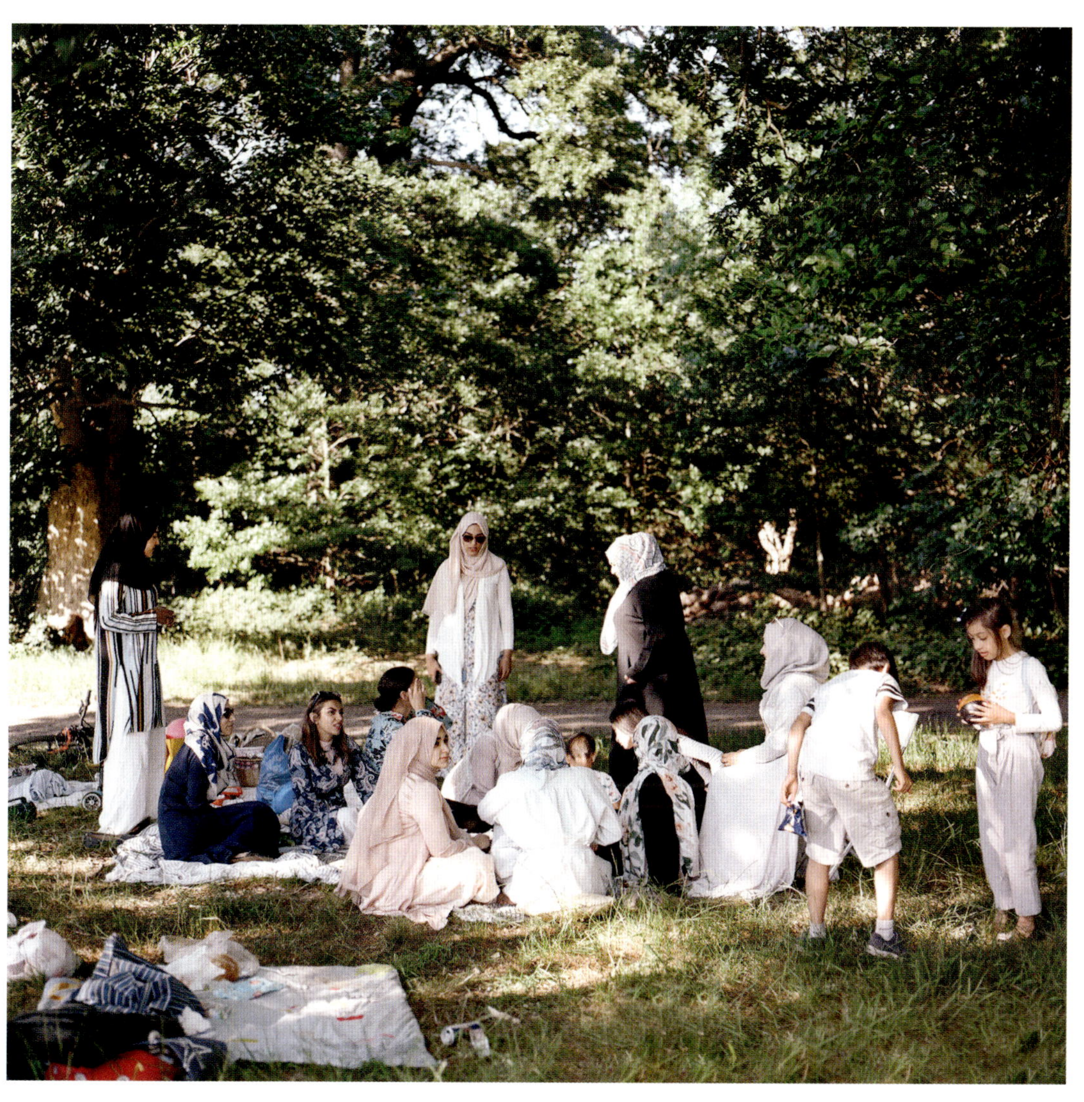

Arzan's baby shower

WANSTEAD PARK

'I only ever really noticed this park during the pandemic,
despite living down the road. It holds a huge significance to me
now; I used to come here every day when I was on furlough
and it offered a sense of peace and tranquillity in the turbulence.'

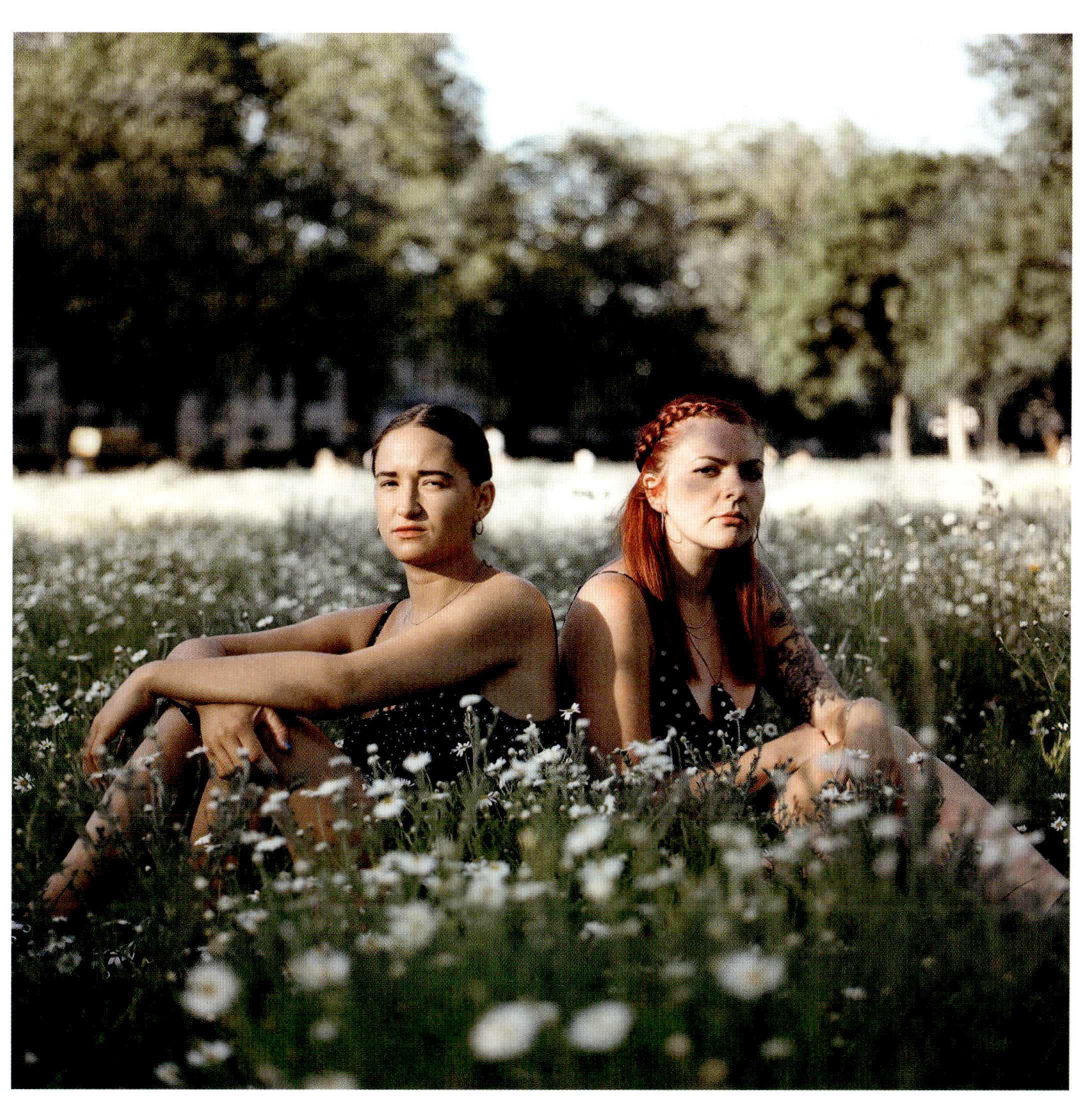

Flora & Chloe

HACKNEY DOWNS

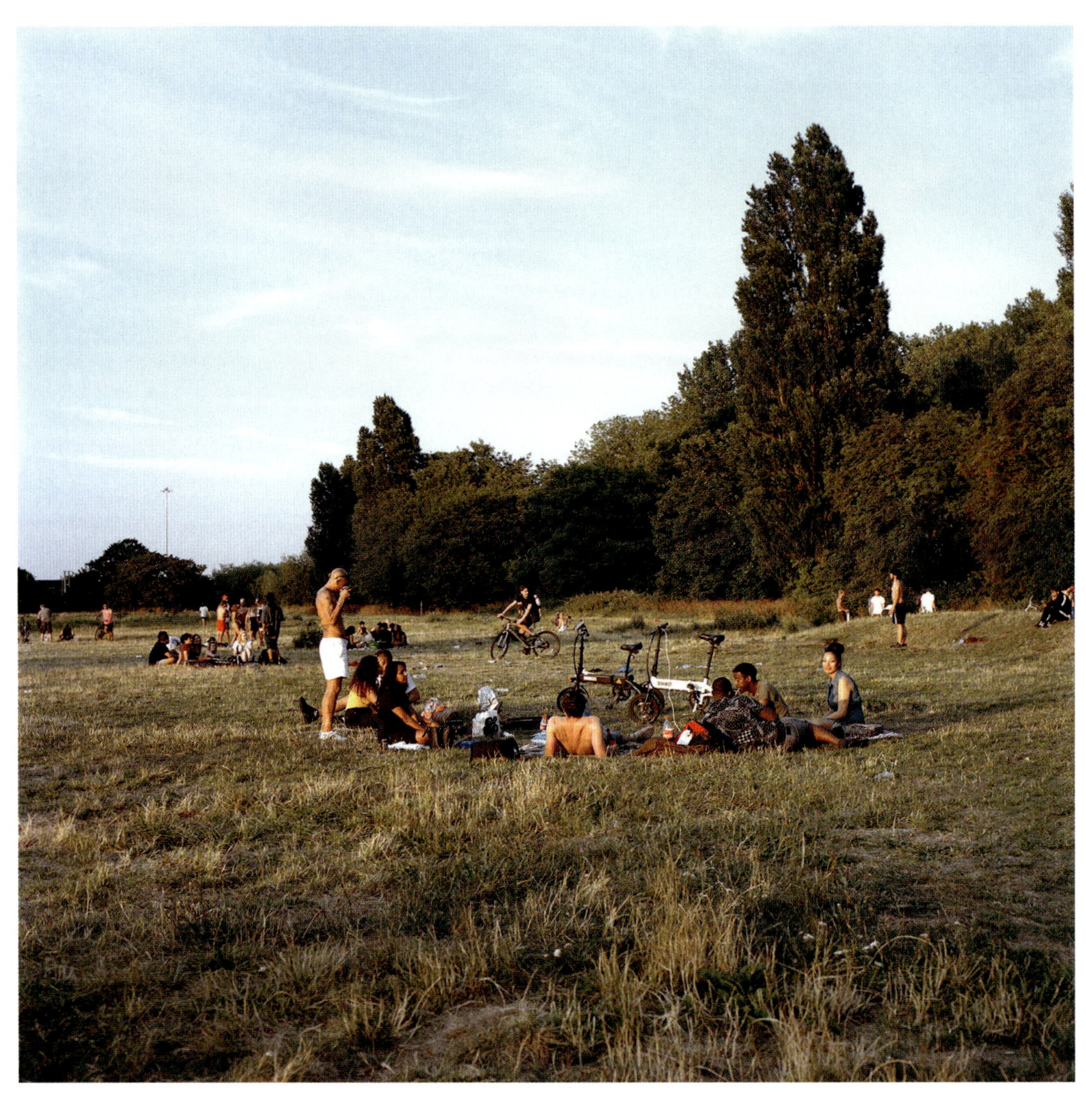

HACKNEY MARSHES

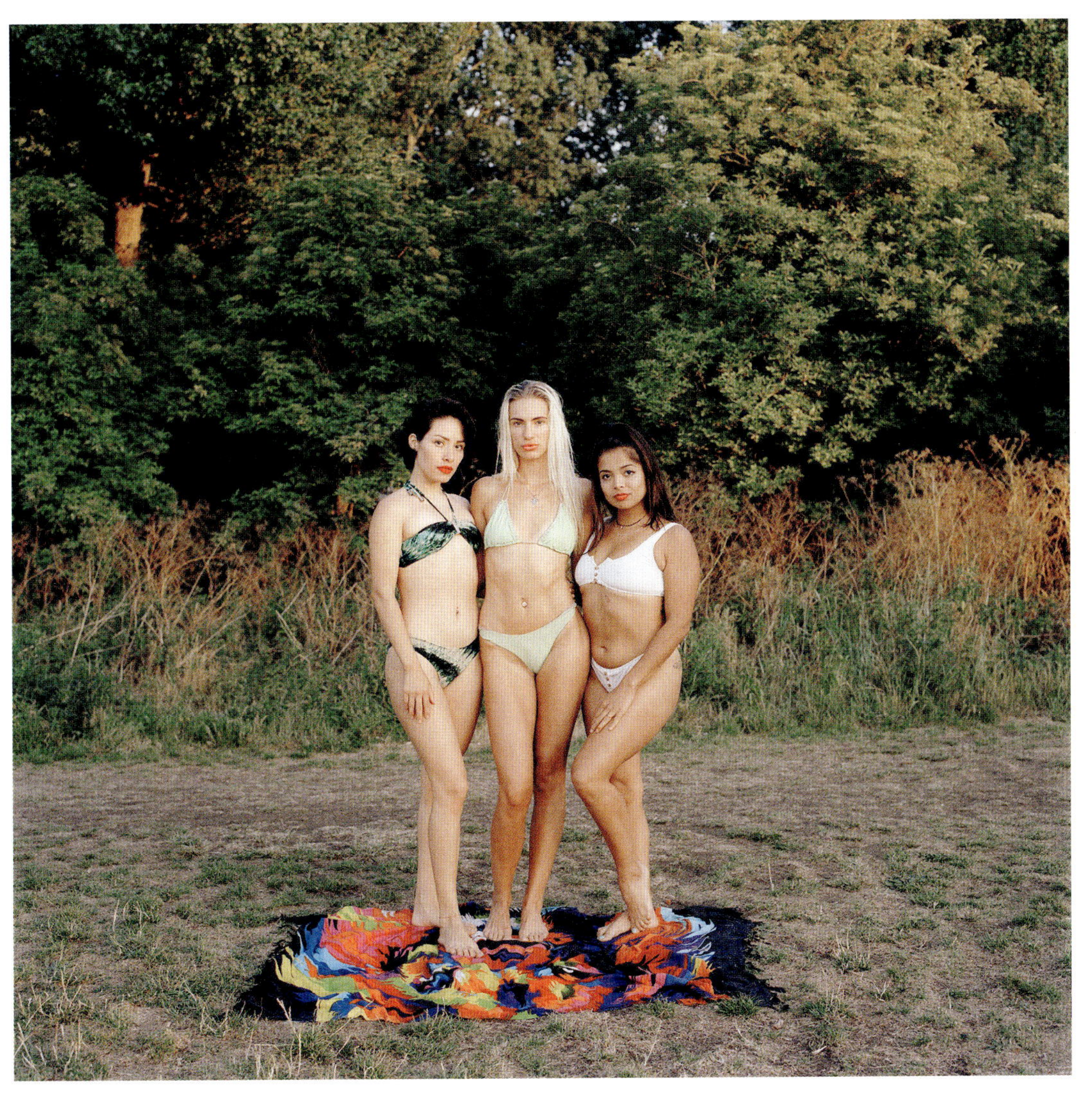

Jennifer, Sophie-Marie & Diana

HACKNEY MARSHES

'I've been coming to Hyde Park all my adult life, but now
at the age of 90 I visit more than ever. When the sun's out I'll bring
a book to read, or I love to just sit in the Rose Garden
and admire the wonderful display of flowers. I'm a painter
so I appreciate colour enormously.'

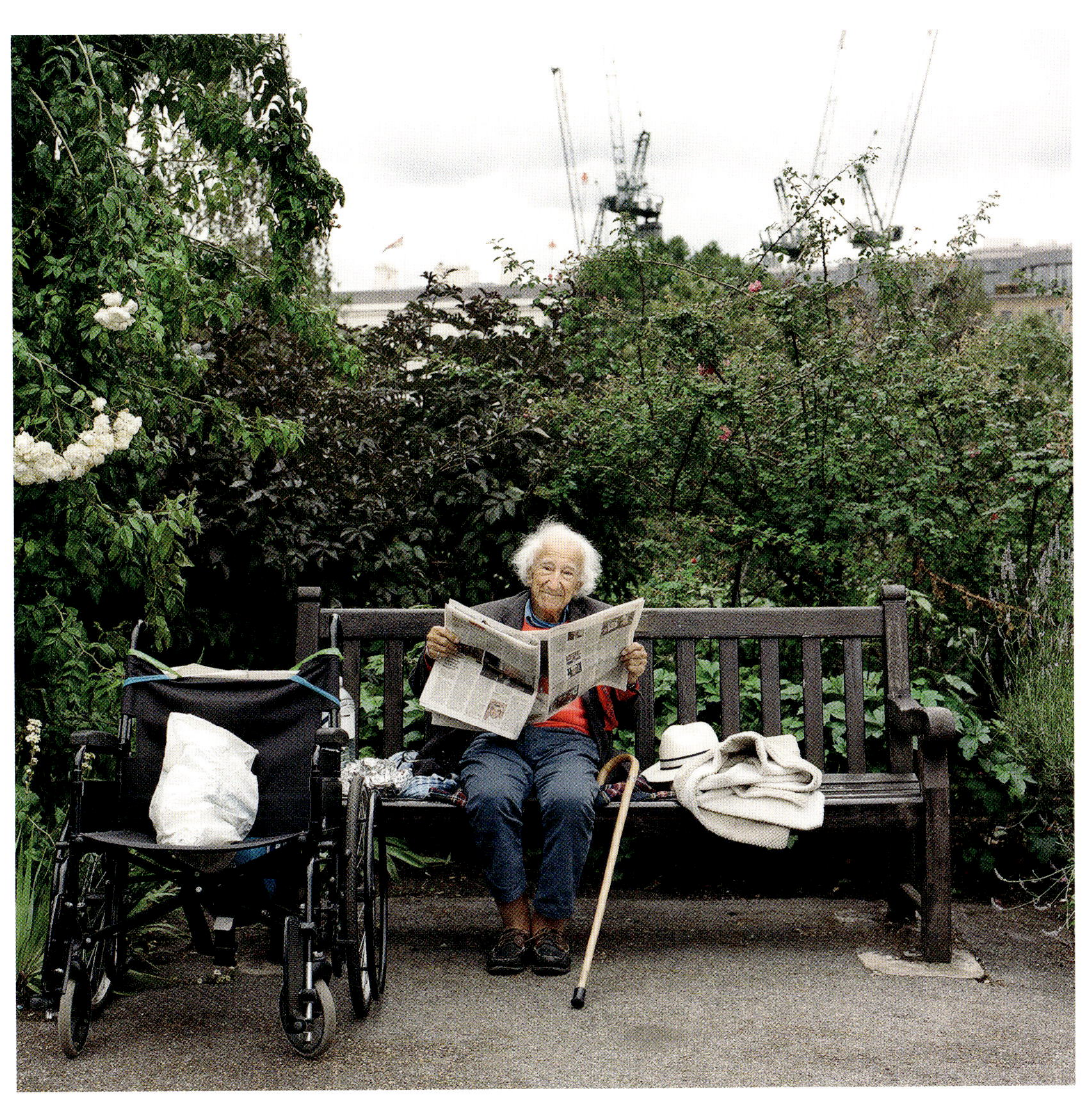

Paul

HYDE PARK

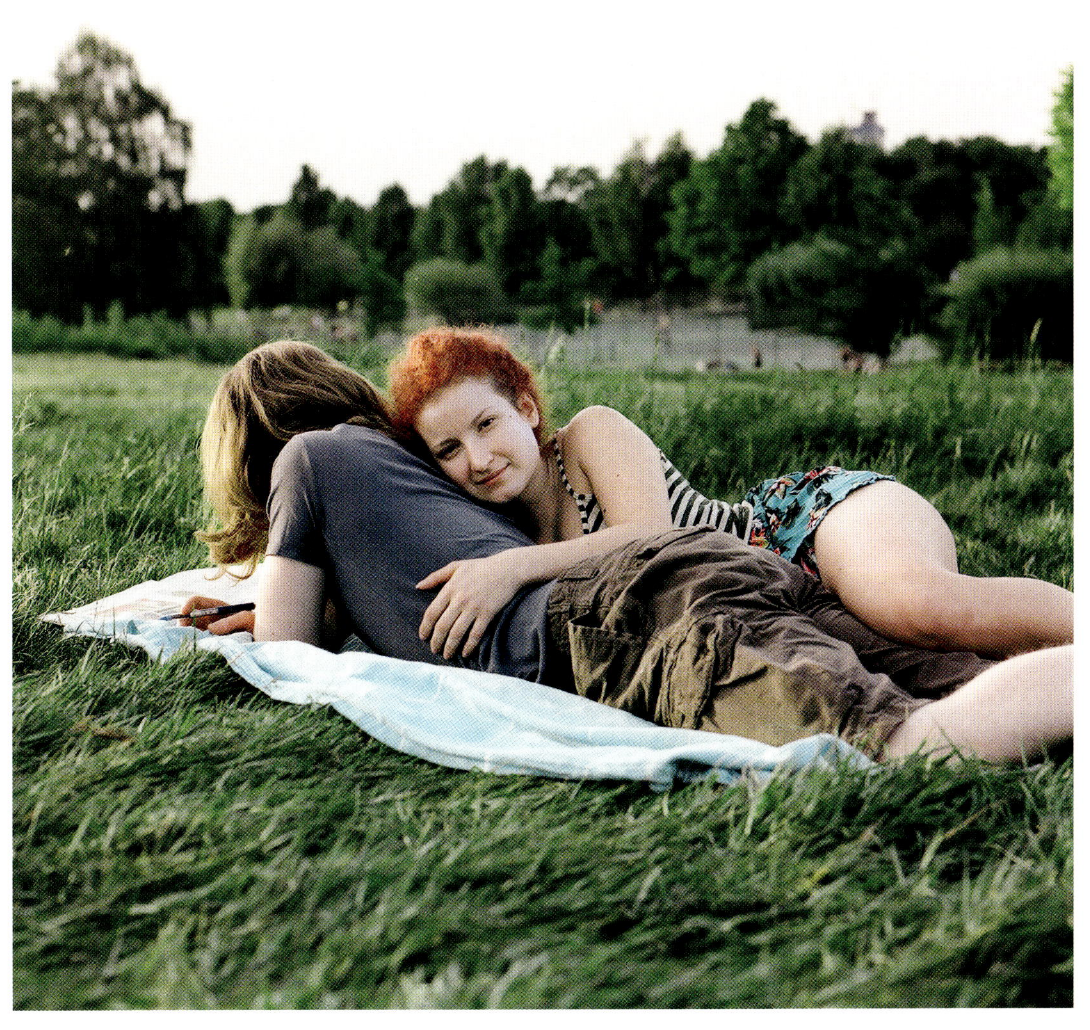

Joe & Natalia

SPRINGFIELD PARK

'I was born in the hospital next to Ruskin Park, so for me
it has a sort of ancient quality, tied up with my very earliest
memories of London and being aware of the city.'

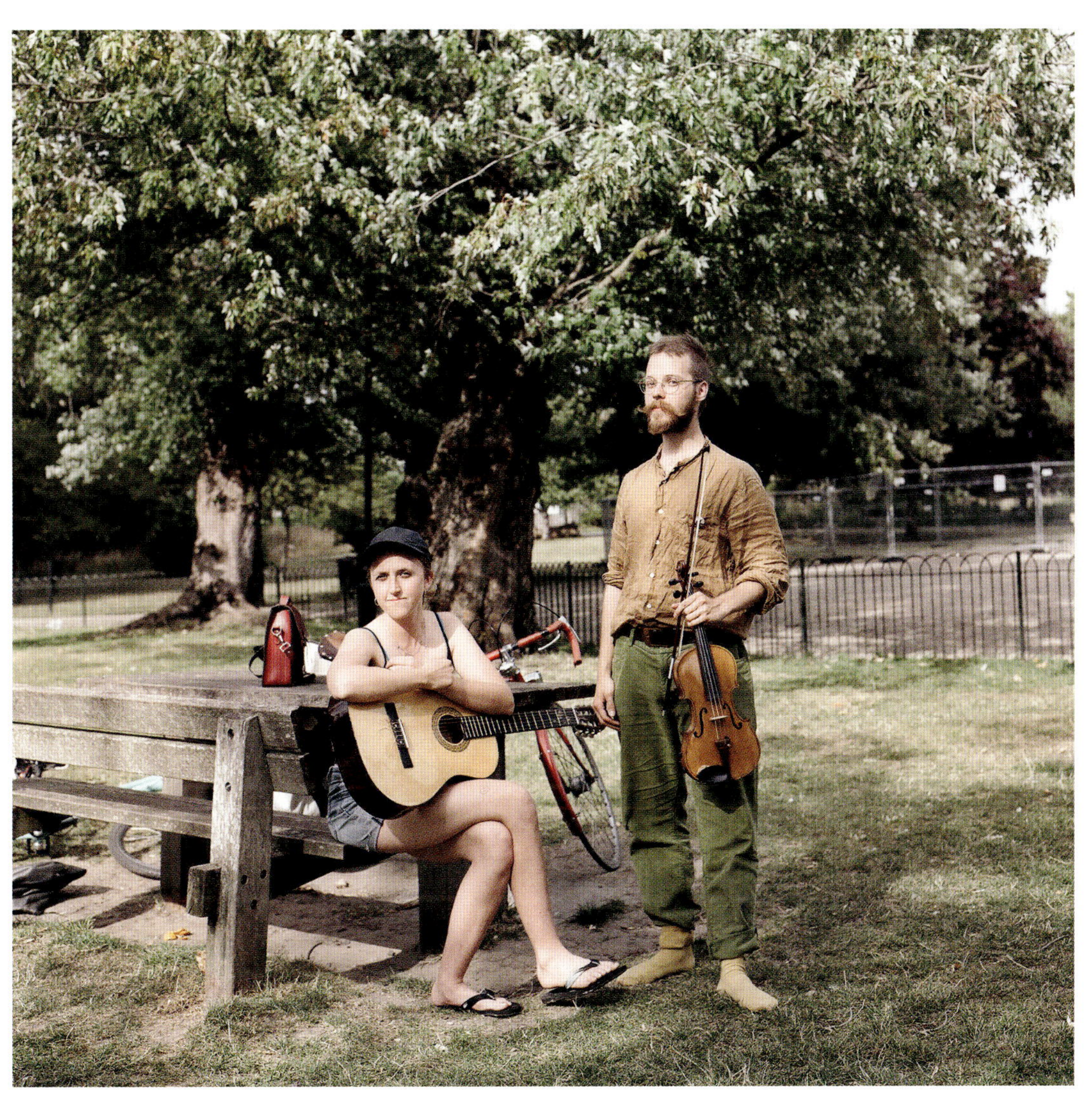

Jess & Seth

RUSKIN PARK

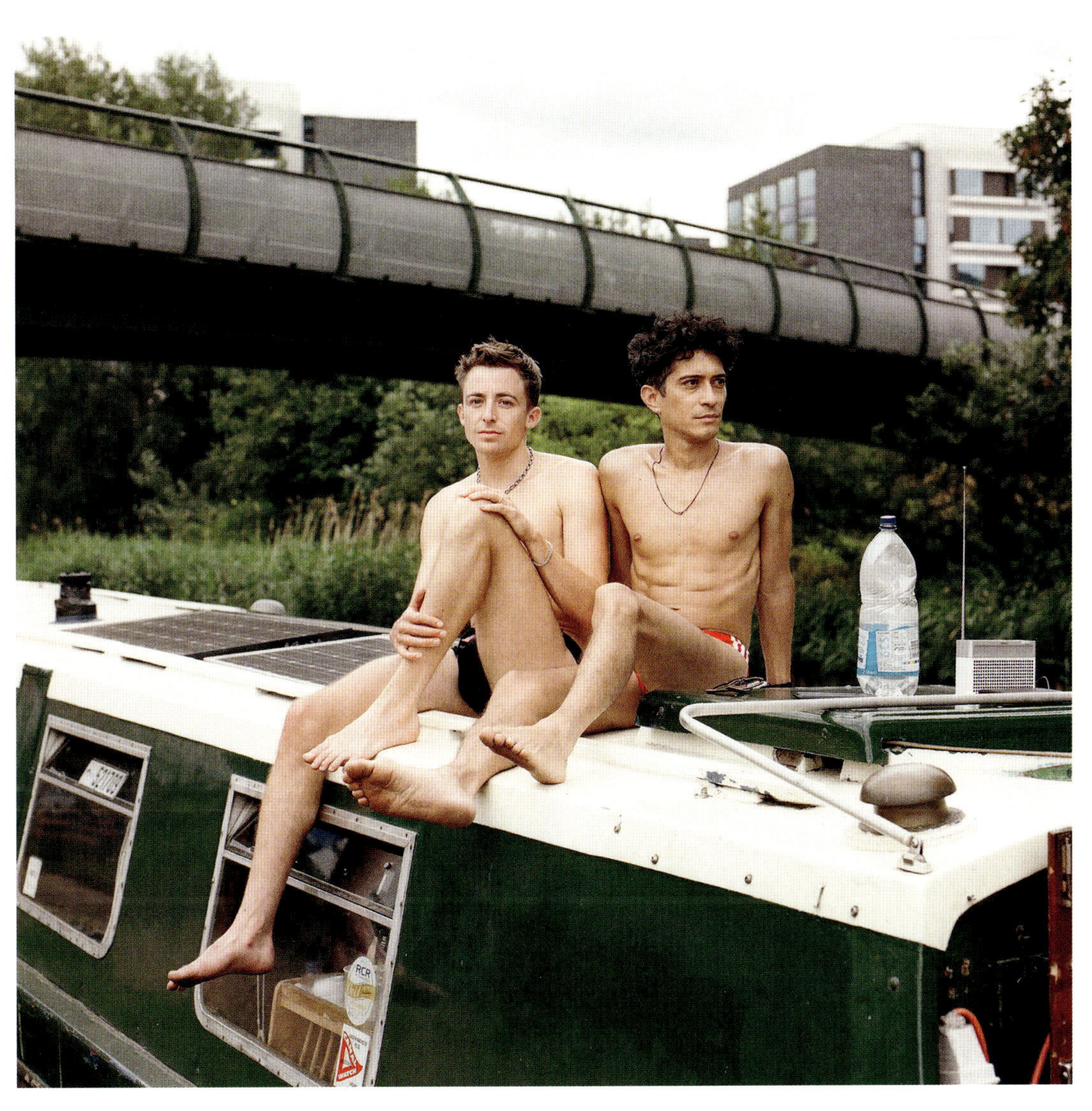

Ben & Gabriel

MILE END PARK

'It's our first link-up in months; we're just catching up
and enjoying each other's company. We all grew up playing in
Shoreditch Park as kids so it's special to be here as adults
on the same soil. I look around and remember all the things we'd
get up to. I live in Essex now, and it just reminds me to never
forget where I came from. Hackney girls rule the world!'

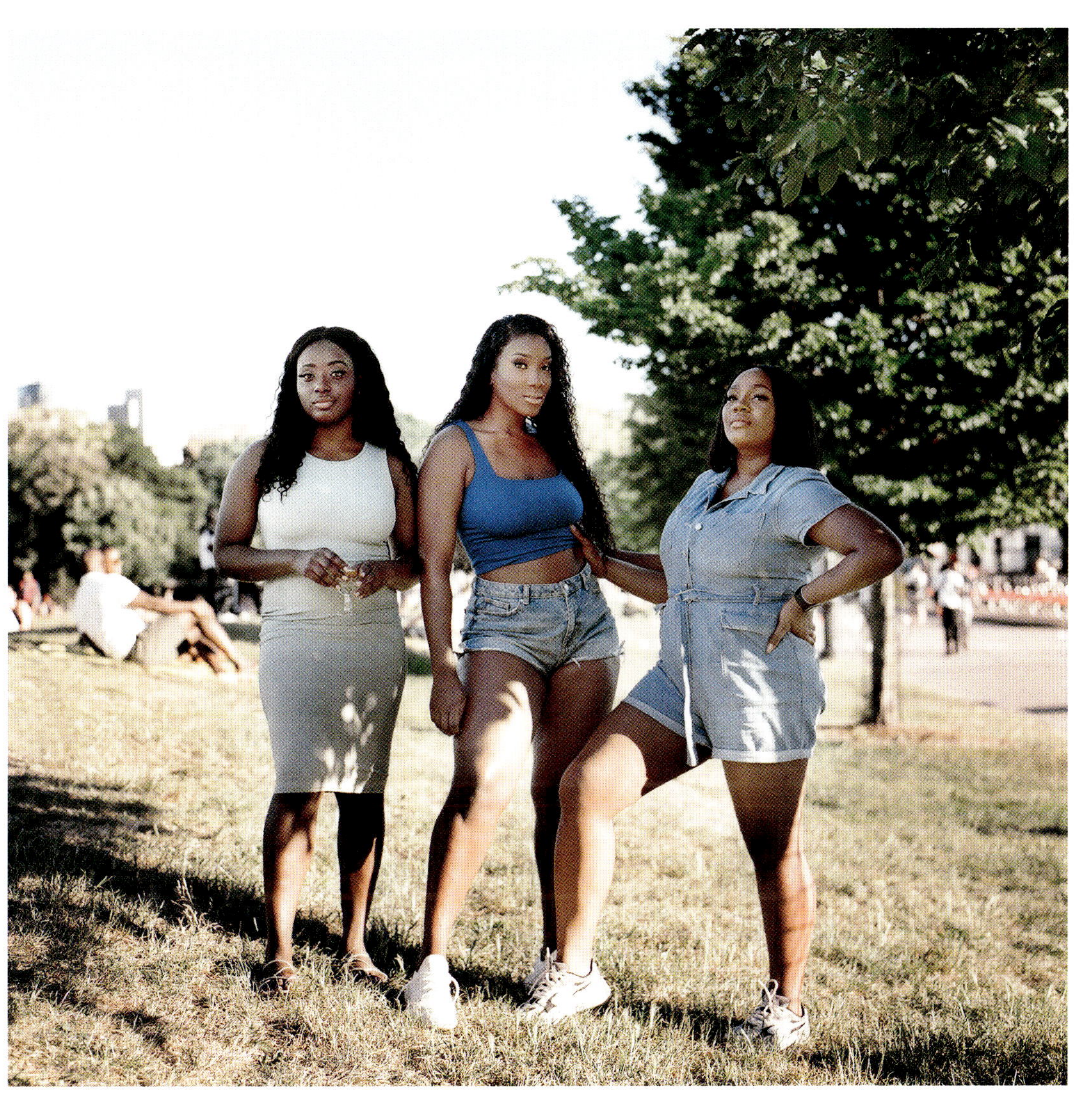

Eleanor, Precious & Anna

SHOREDITCH PARK

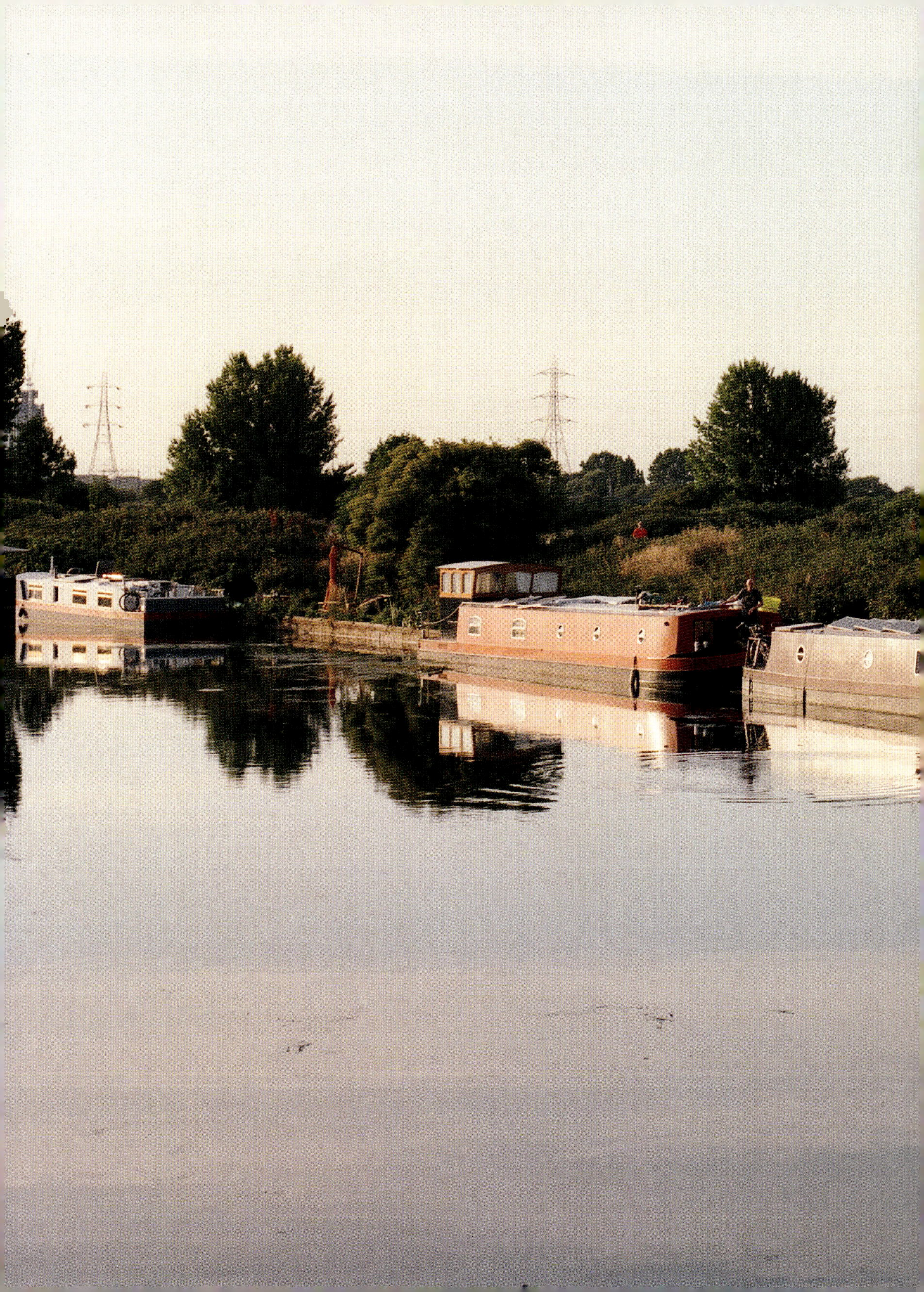

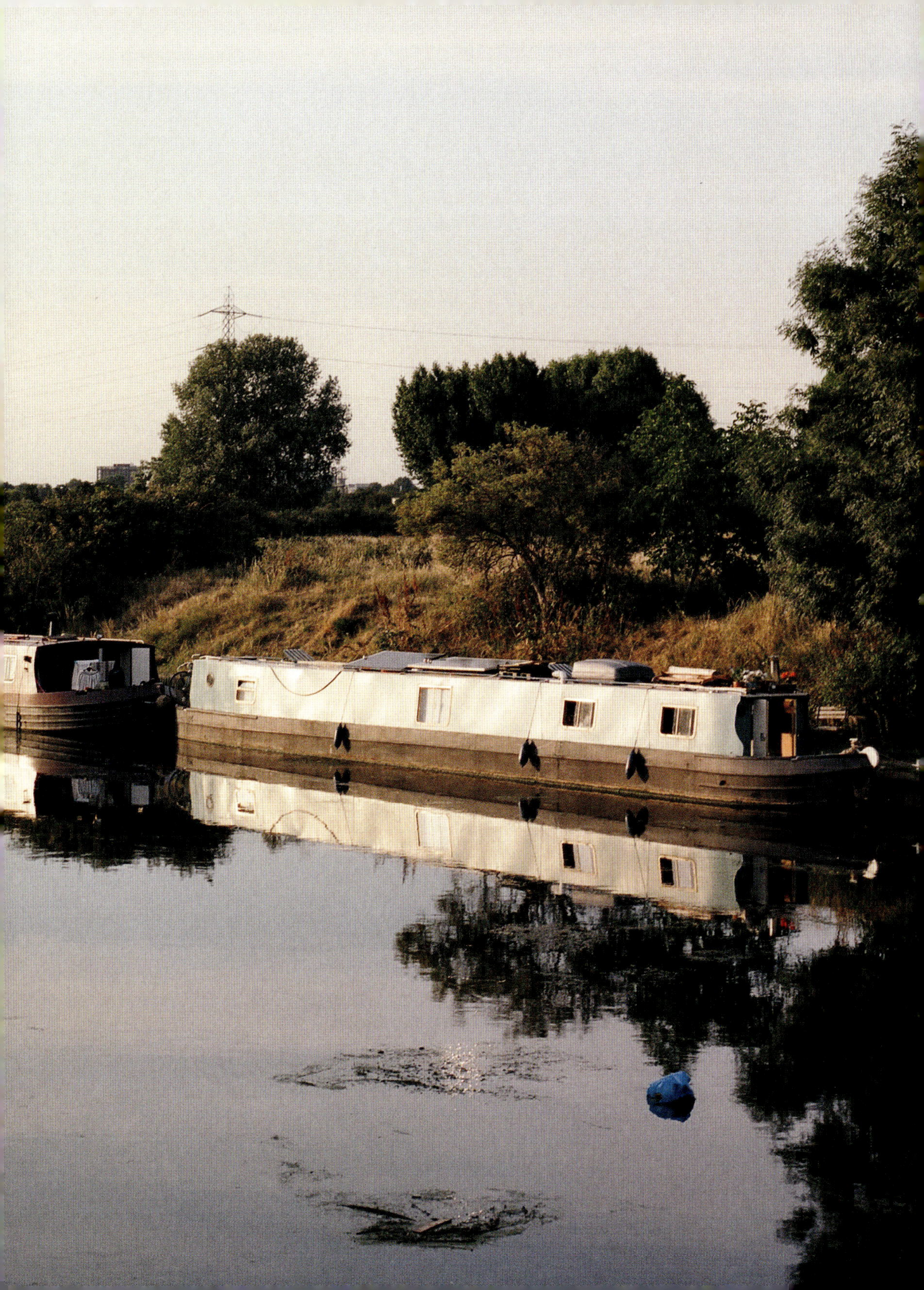

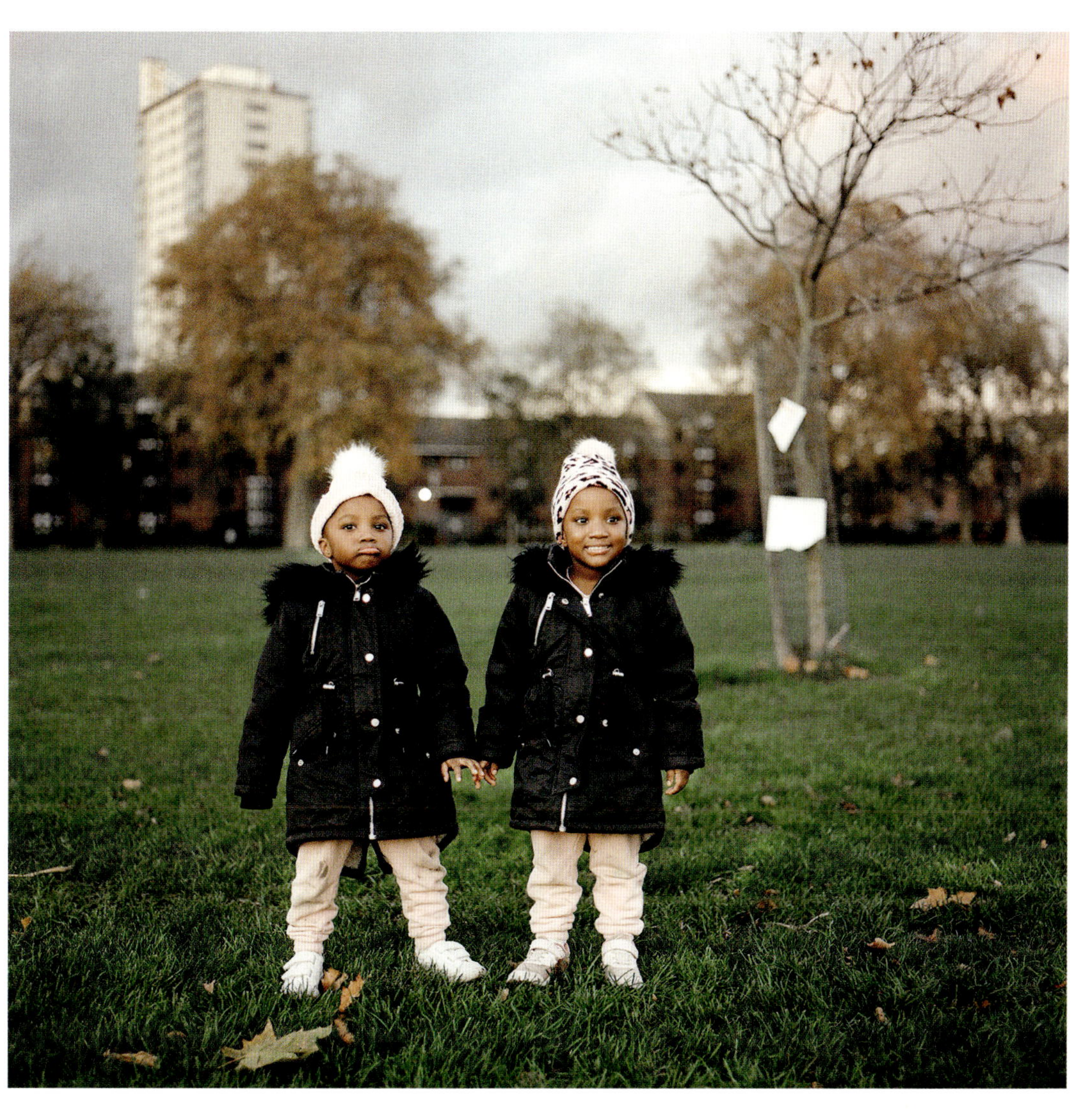

Venus & Honey

HACKNEY DOWNS

'I often think about William Blake when I visit Peckham Rye. He had a vision here of angels in an oak tree, with "bright angelic wings bespangling every bough like stars." It's amazing to think he walked in the same places I do.'

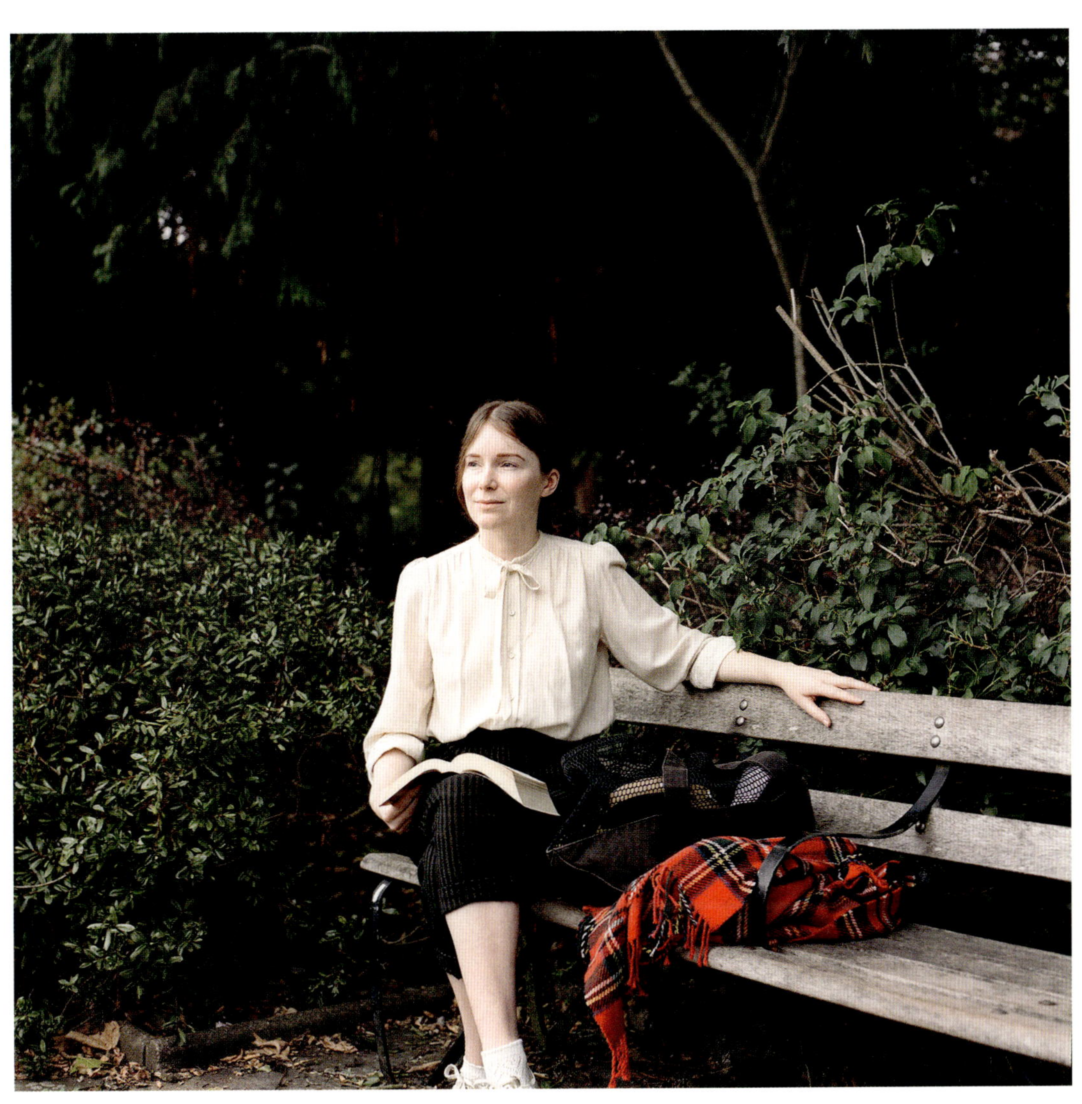

Hannah

PECKHAM RYE

'Walking through Highgate Wood is a form of meditation for me. When I'm among the trees, I'm able to turn down the volume on my thoughts.'

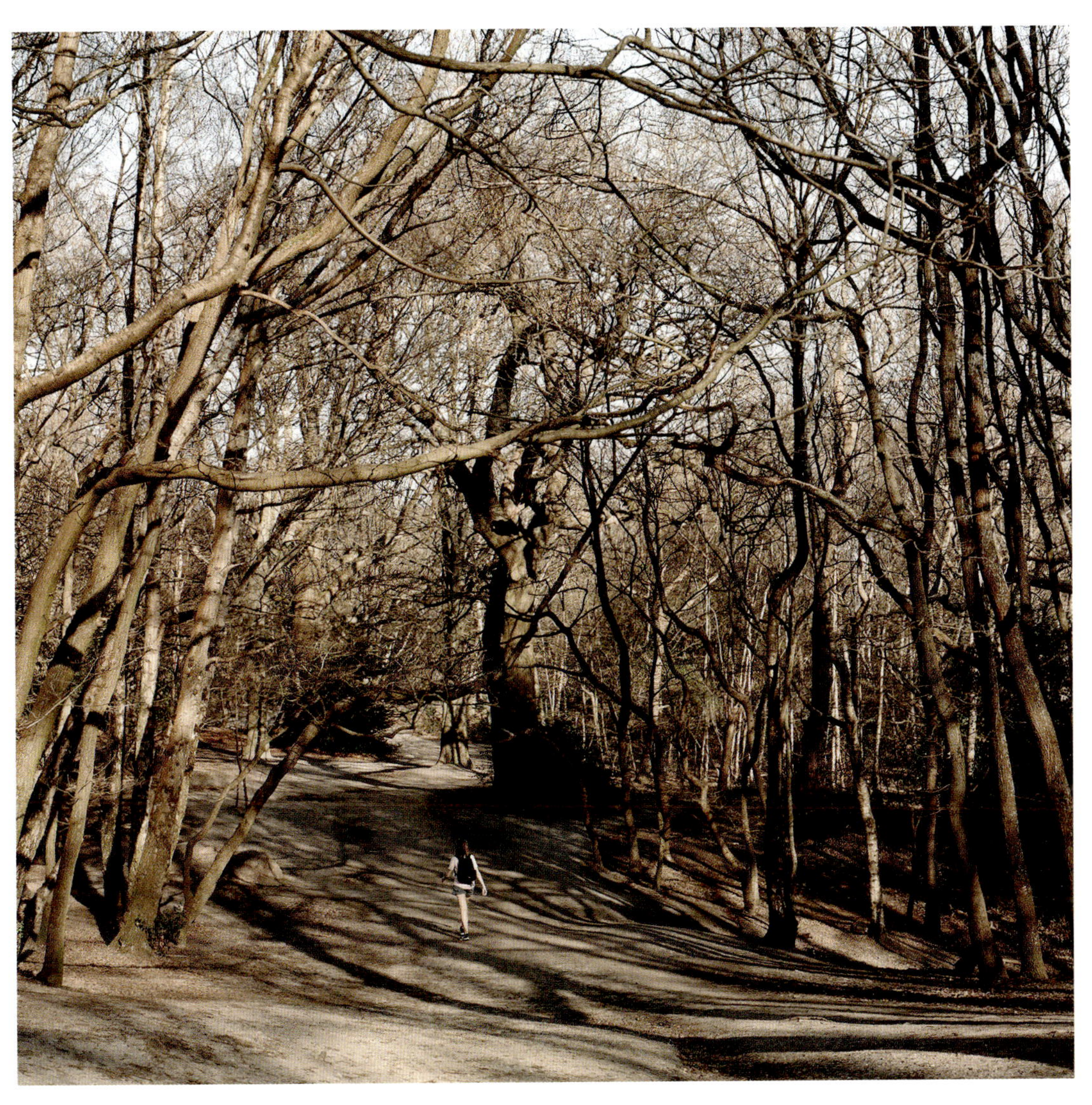

Stella

HIGHGATE WOOD

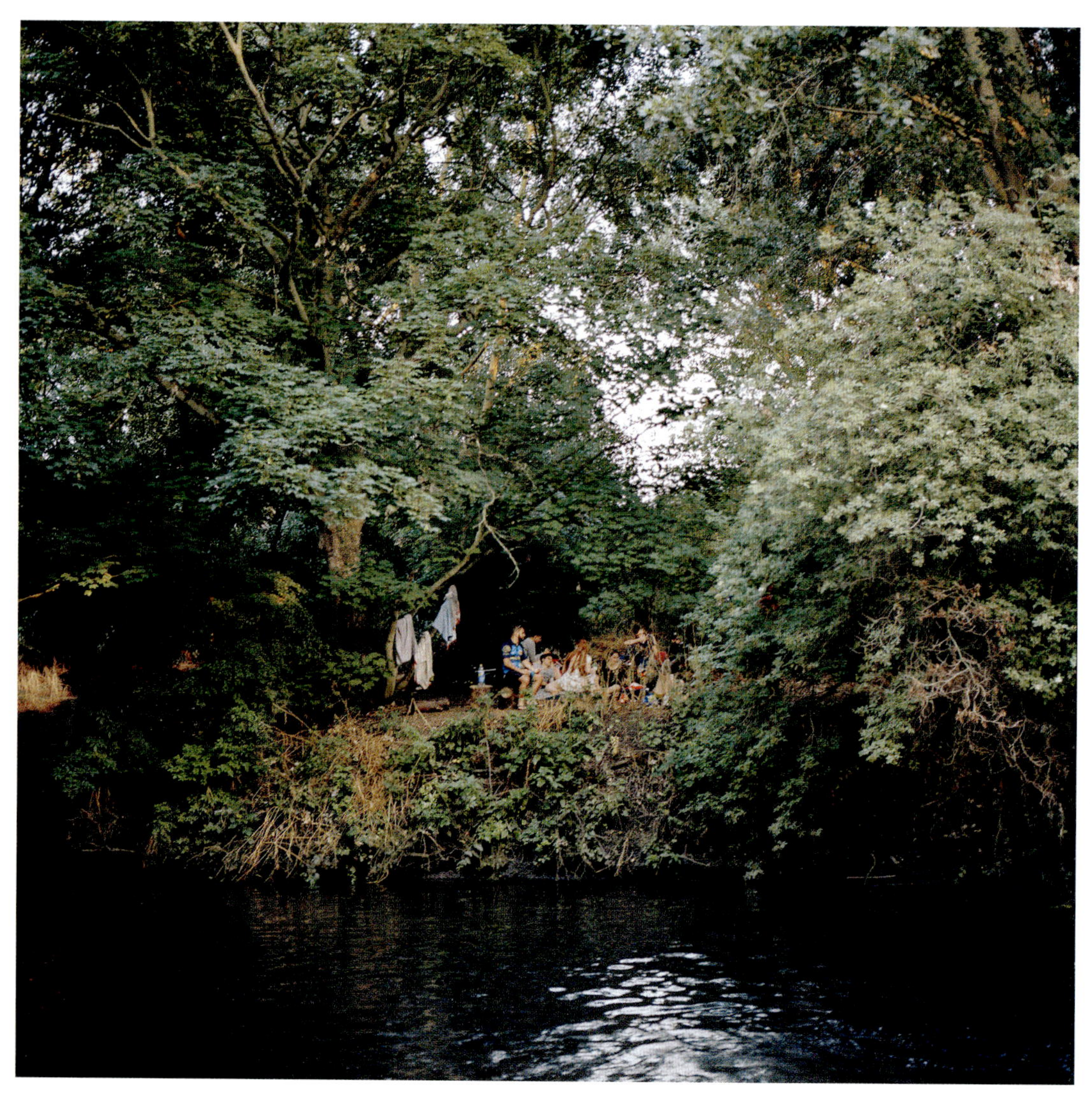

RIVER LEA

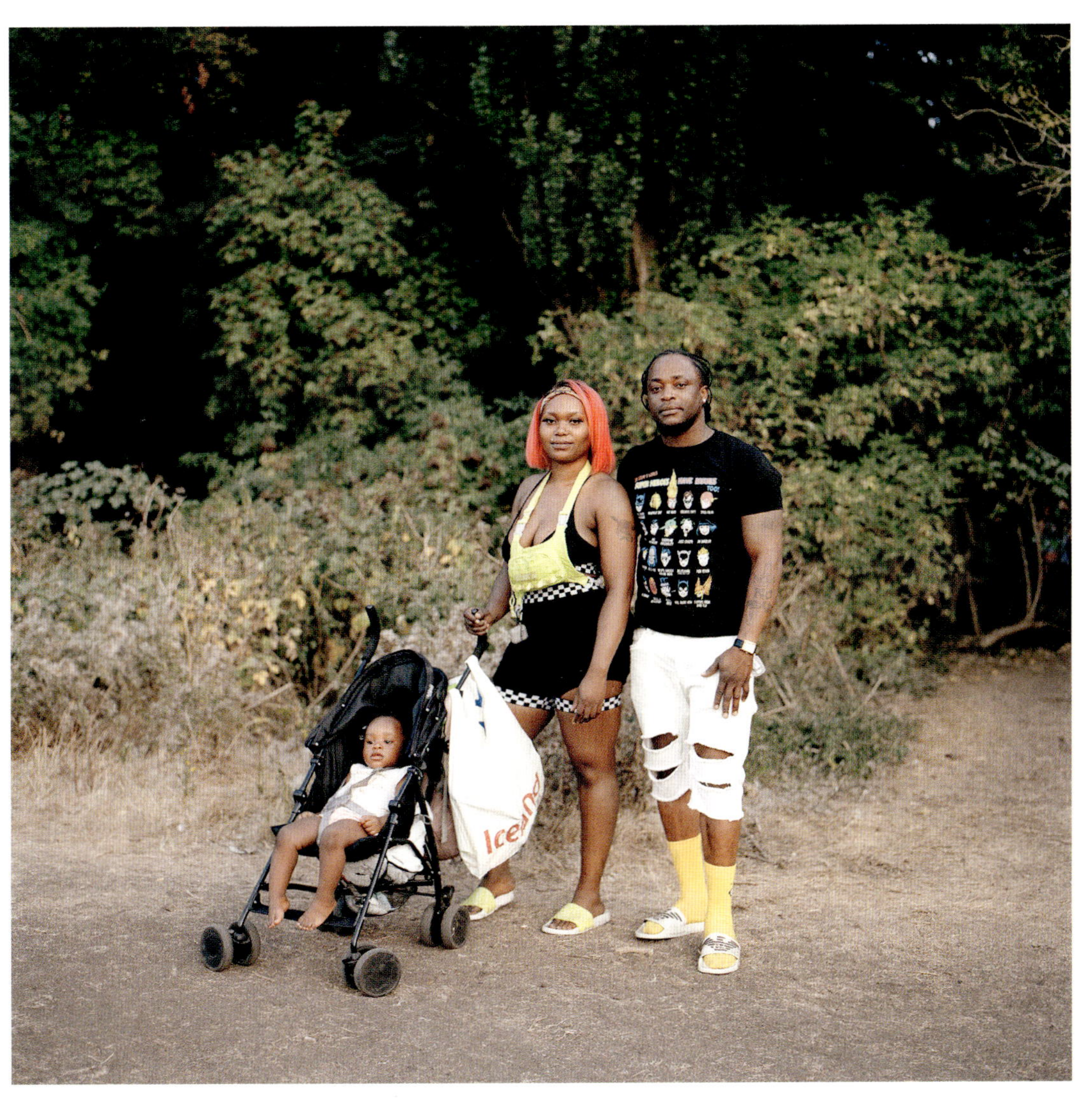

Jade, Janae & Jermaine

HACKNEY MARSHES

'I love going into nature and simply chilling in silence,
it makes me feel "connected" – I'm not sure exactly what it is
that I feel connected to, but I love that feeling.'

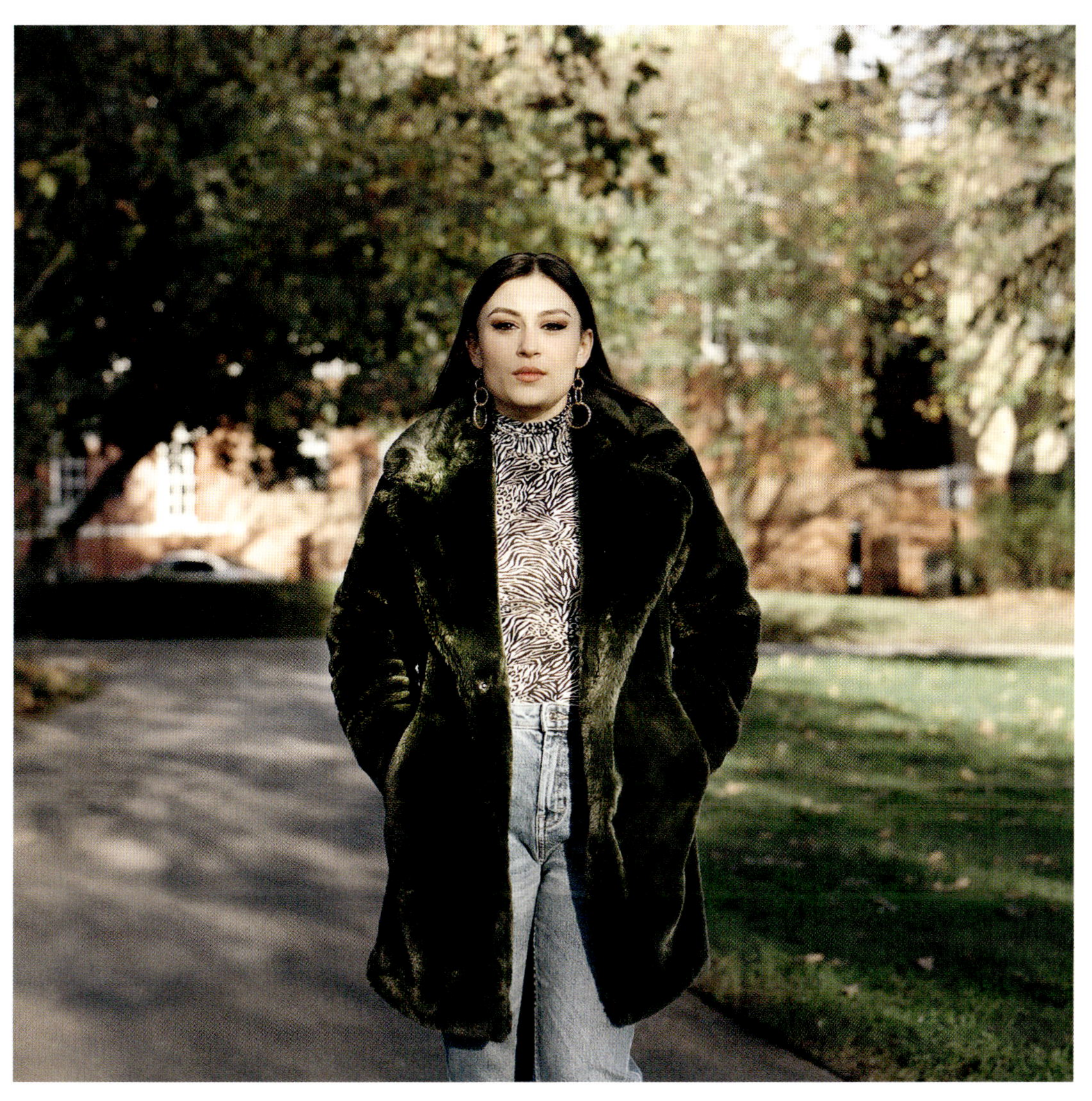

Gamze

ST JOHN-AT-HACKNEY CHURCHYARD GARDENS

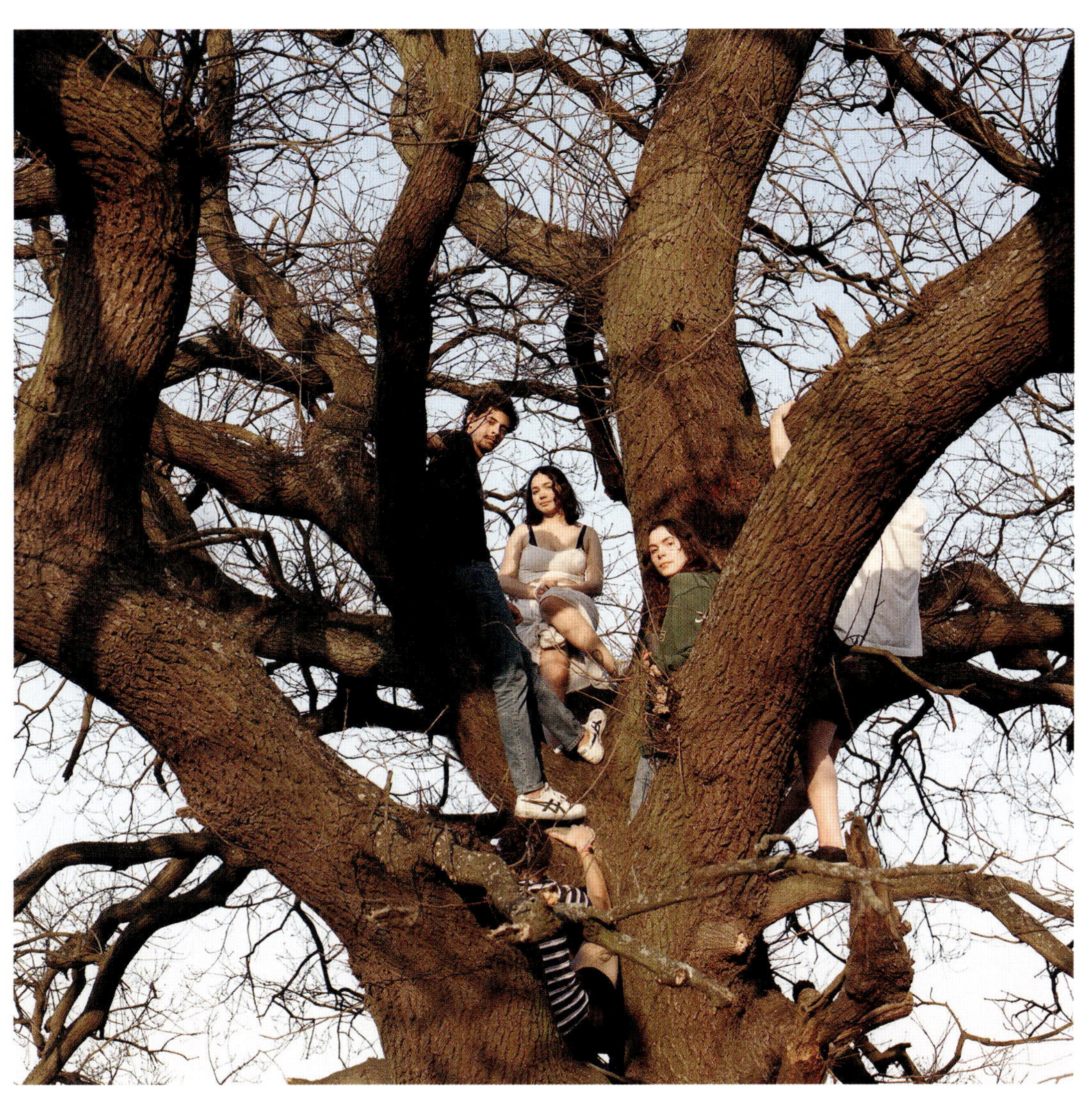

Rafael, Regina & Elena
HAMPSTEAD HEATH

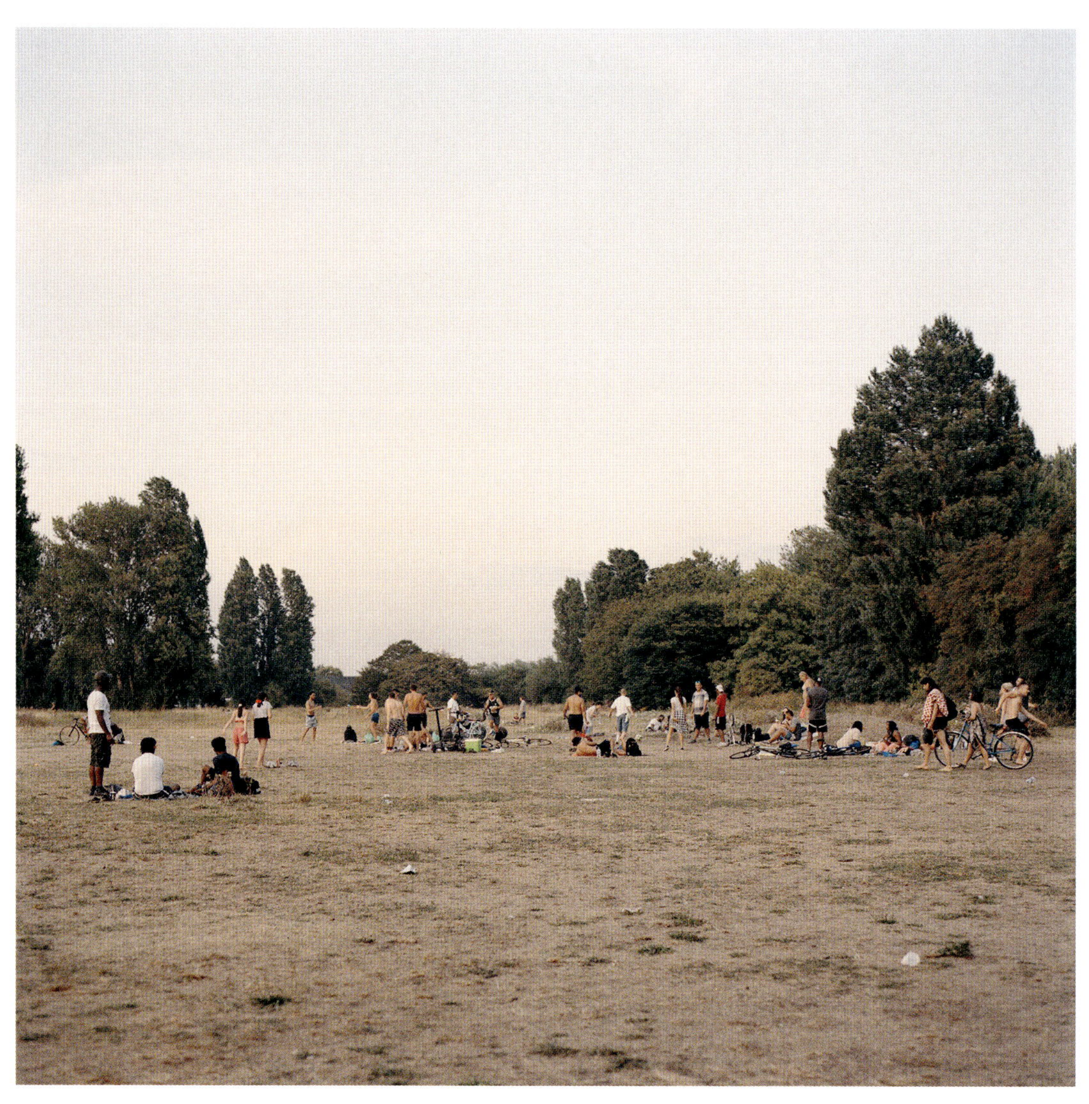

LEE VALLEY PARK

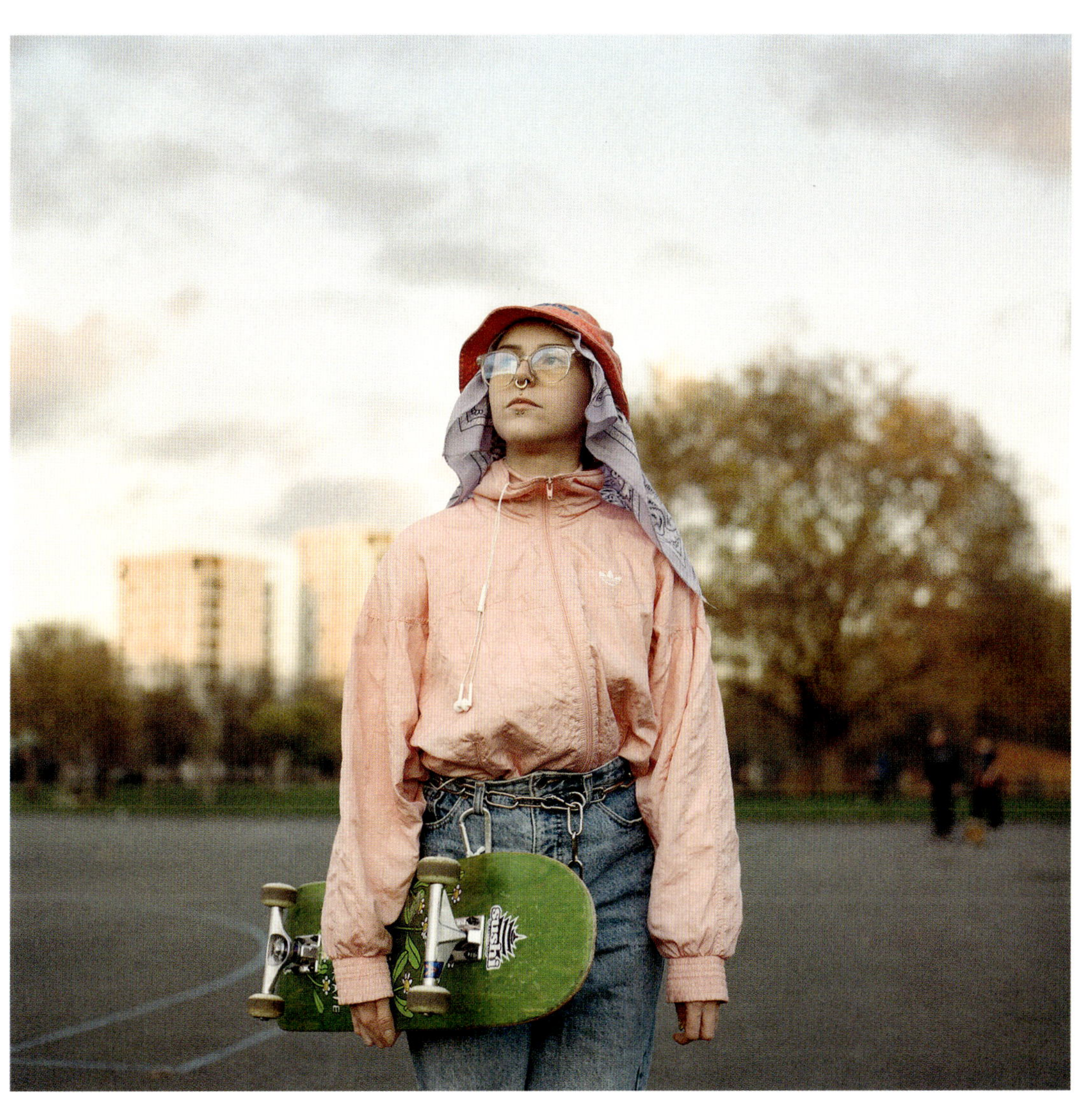

Clarry

VICTORIA PARK

‘London is a city with as many trees as there are people.
I feel lucky to live here.’

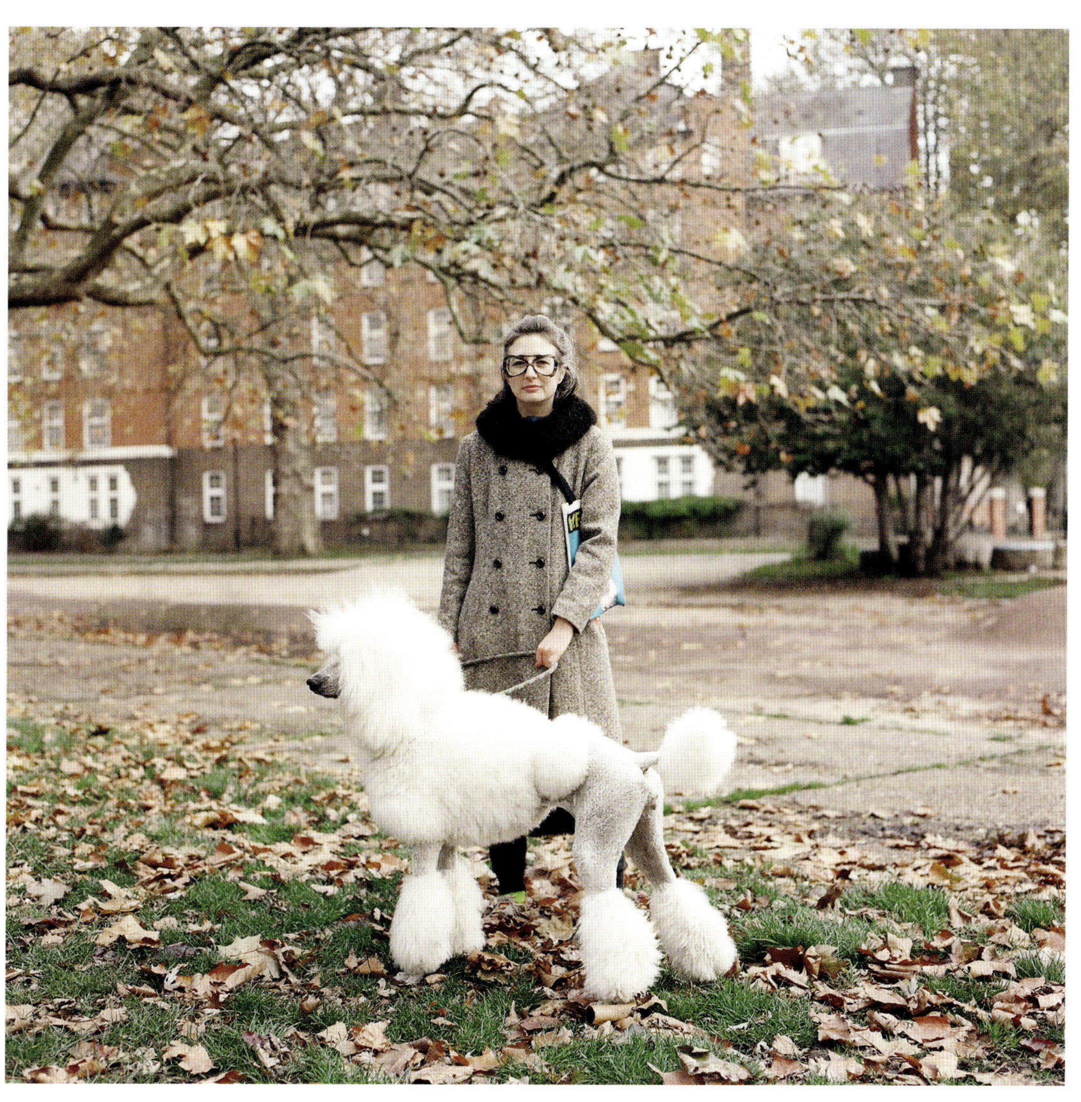

Sara & Rei

LONDON FIELDS

'Kenwood and Hampstead Heath are such special places for us.
We're not London natives but both our little girls were
born in Camden and have lived in north London all their lives.
People often say London is built up, overpopulated and
polluted, but it feels gloriously untamed here.'

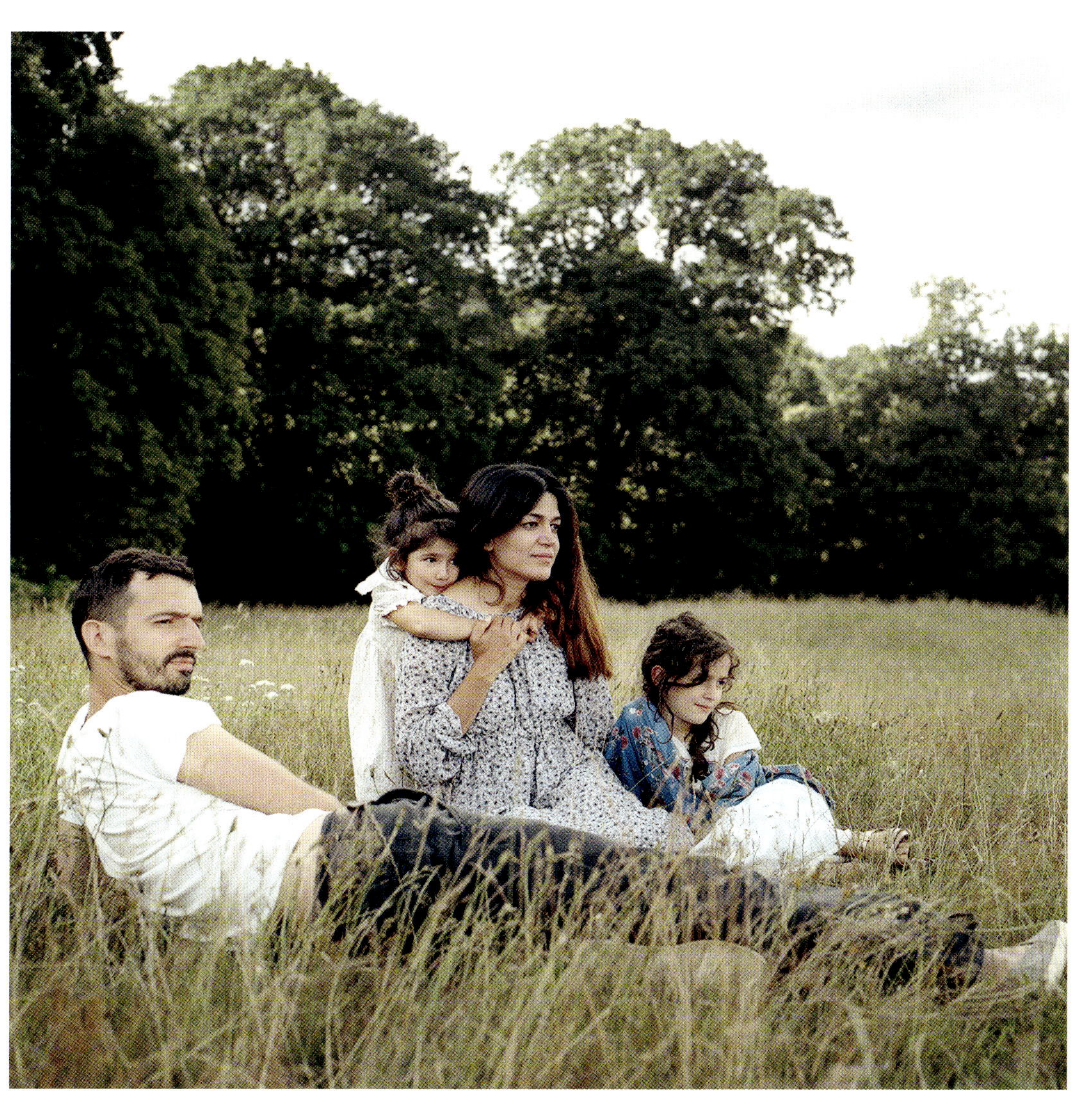

Joe, Madhis, Evie & Minou

KENWOOD PARK

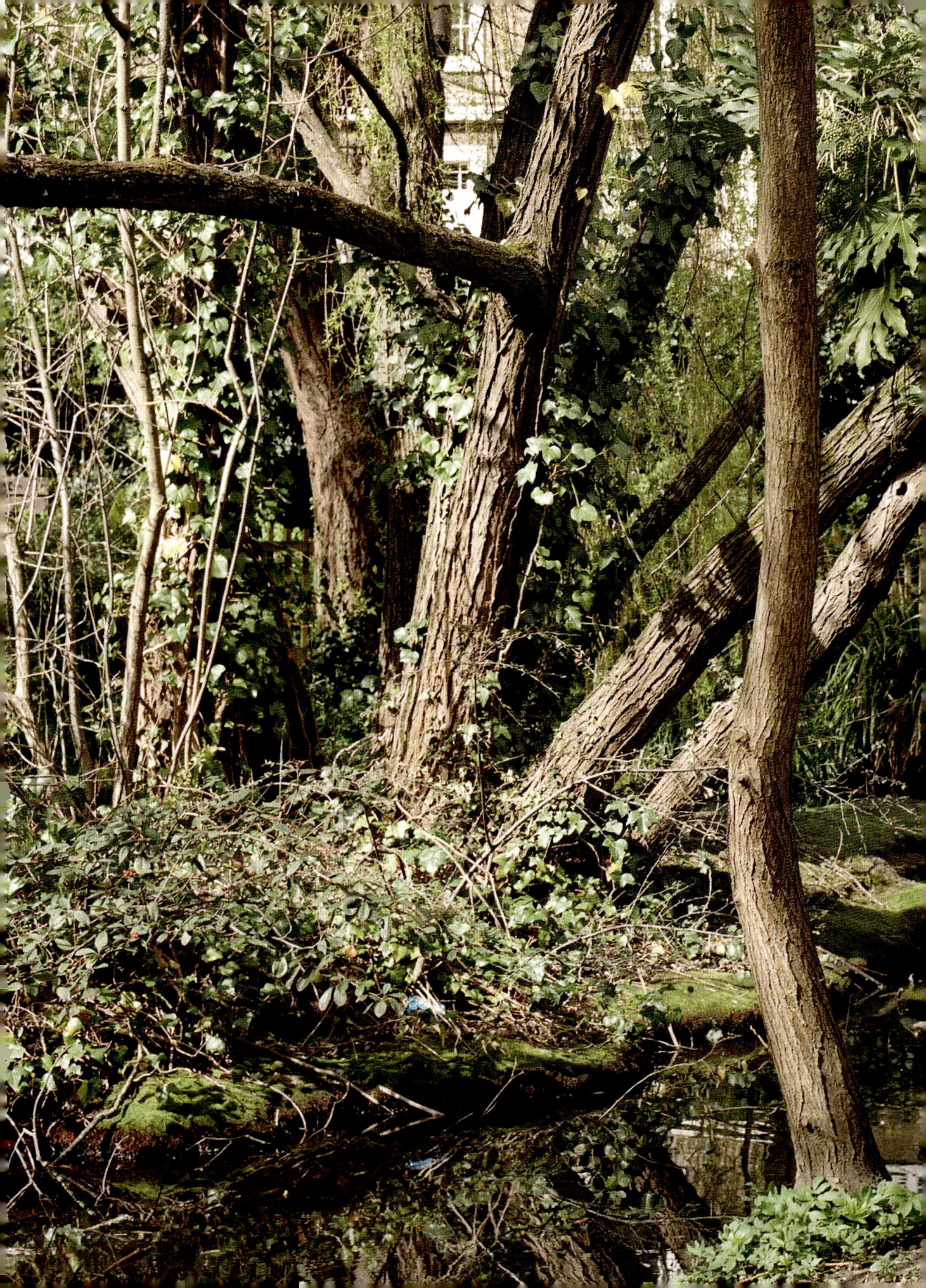

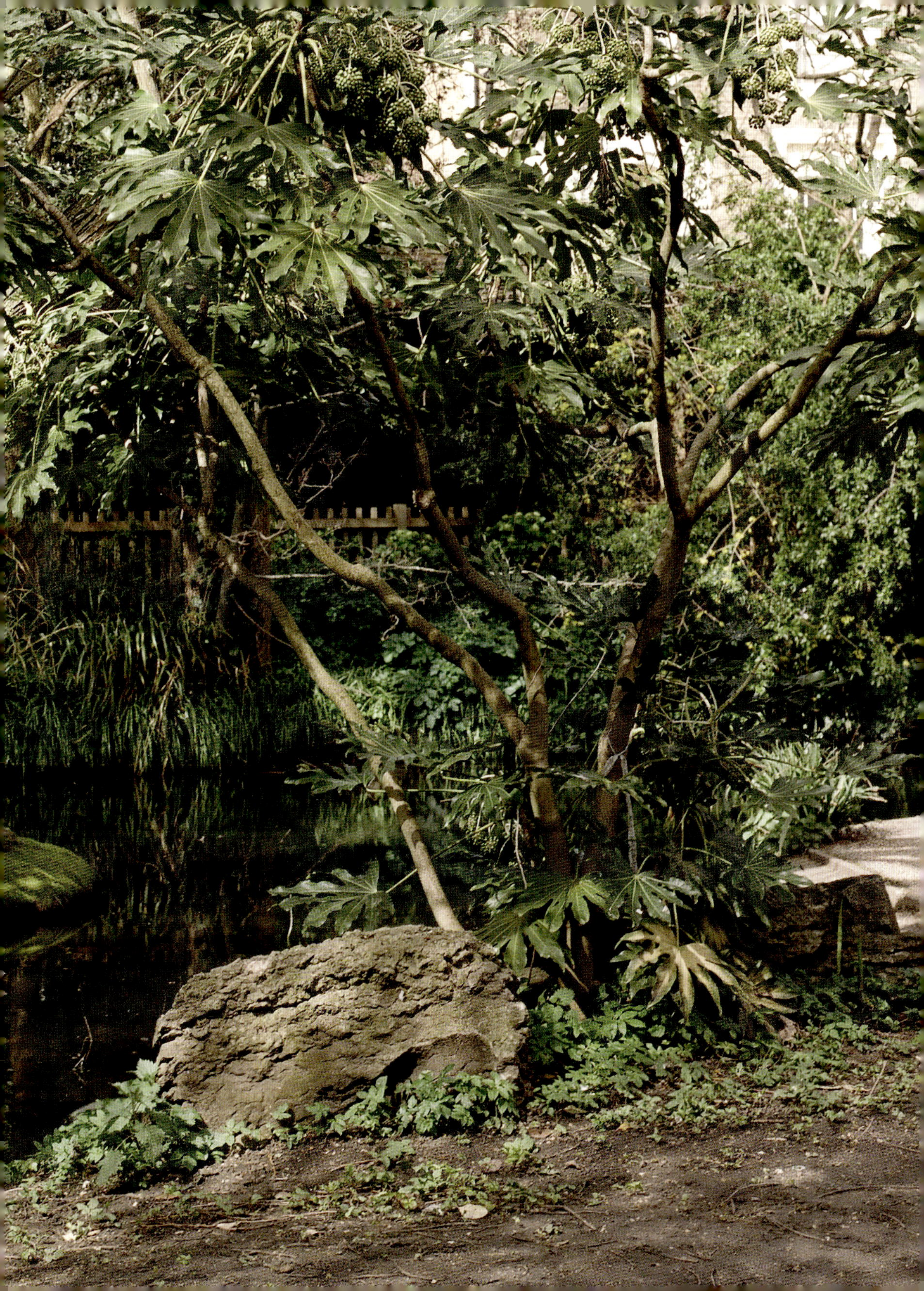

'This is the place where we all learnt to ride our bikes, scooters
and skateboards. We've even been to parties here. We're all
born and bred in Hackney and its green spaces mean a lot to us,
even this one, which is probably one of the smallest.'

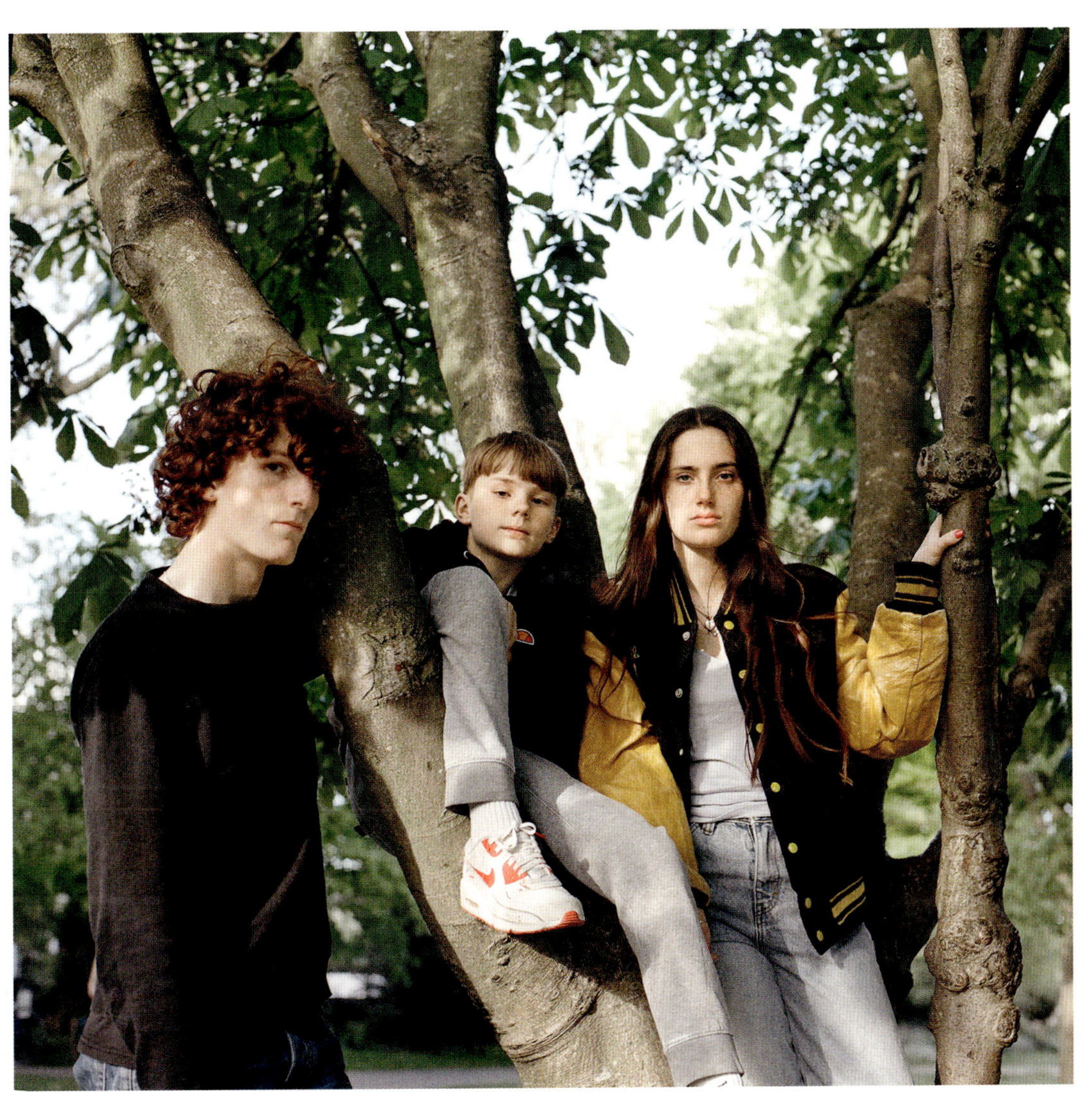

Lucien, Rufus & Lola

WEST HACKNEY RECREATION GROUND

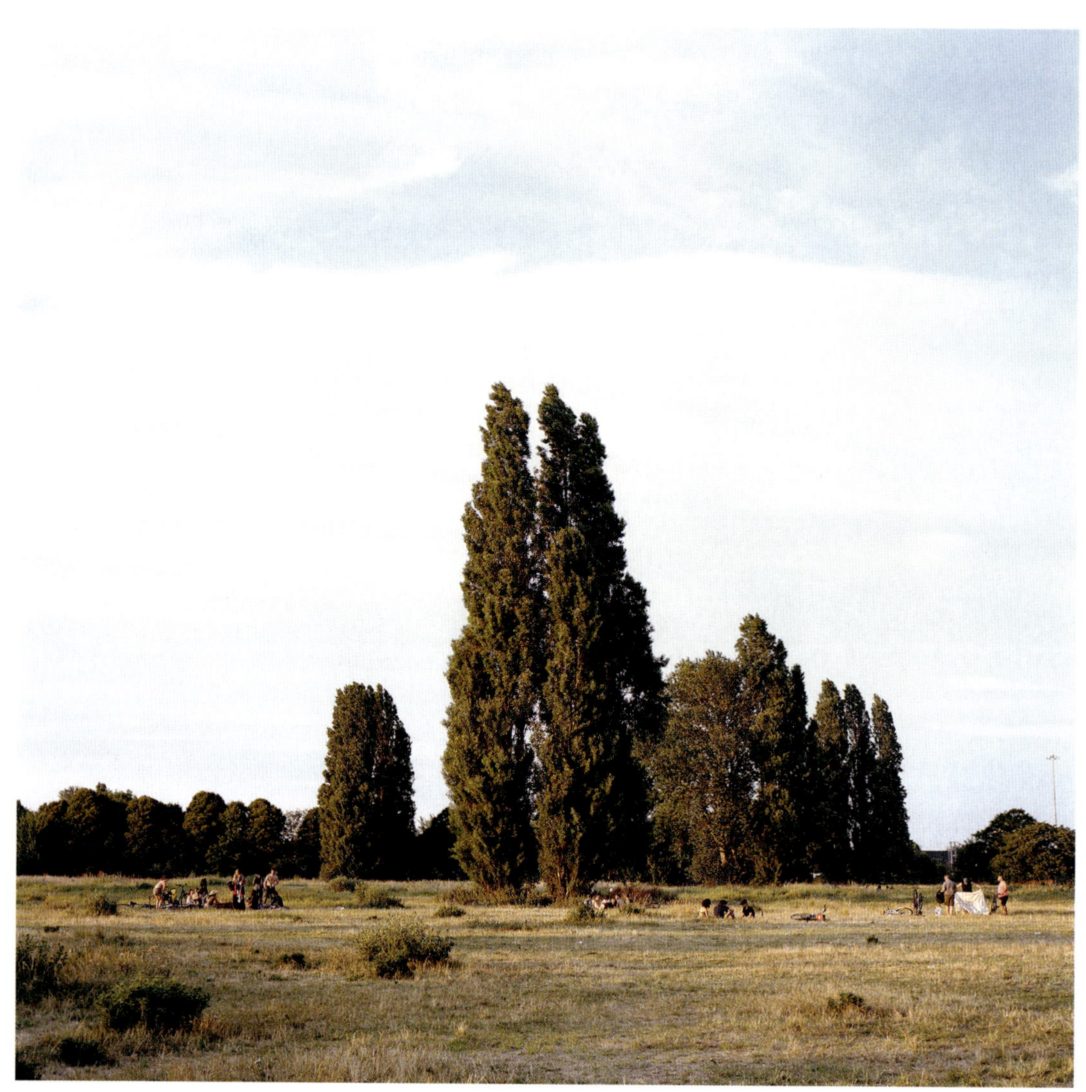

HACKNEY MARSHES

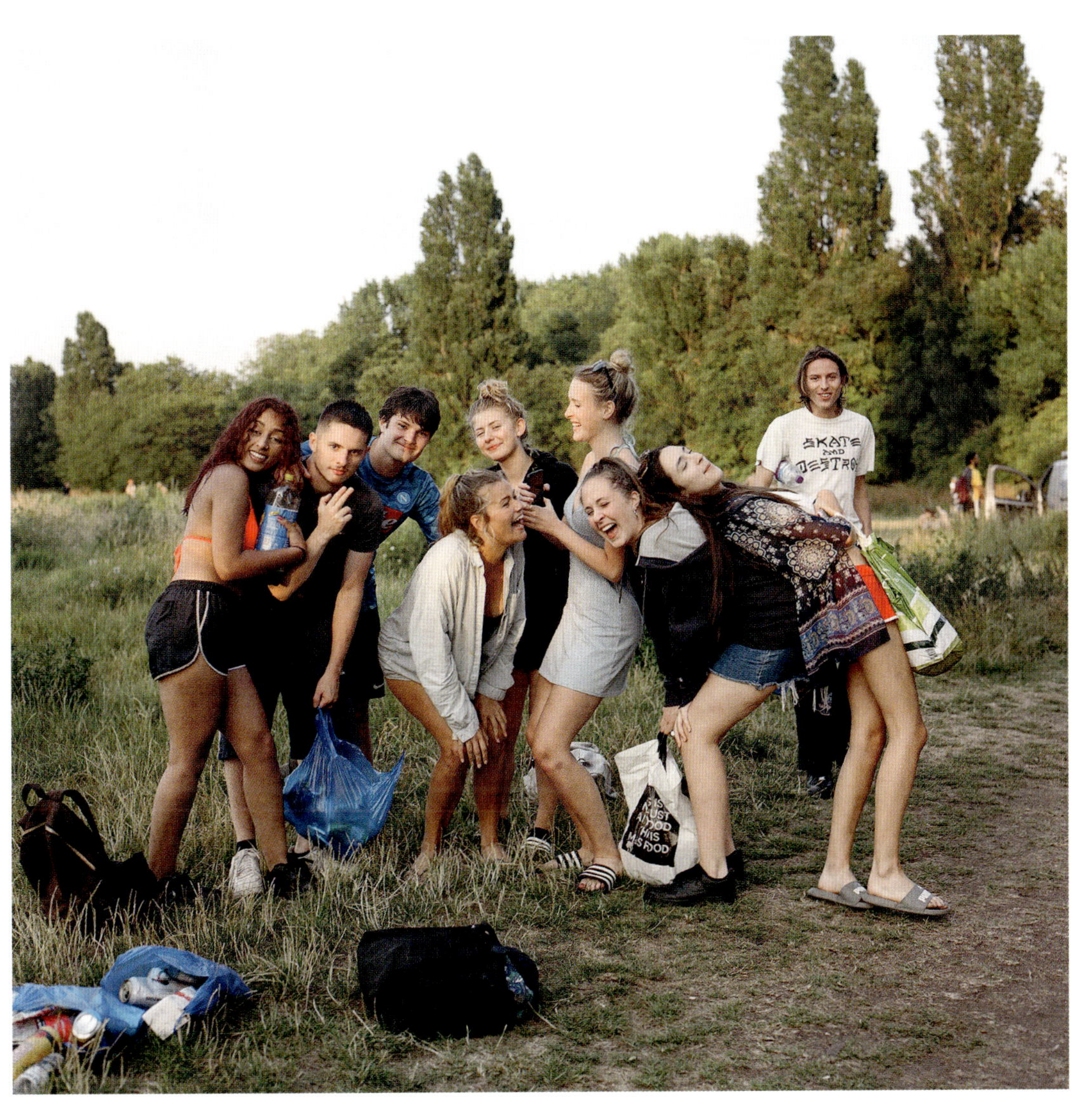

Lolly, Kieran, Scott, Nancy, Katie, Holly, Hope, Zahrah & Louis
LEE VALLEY PARK

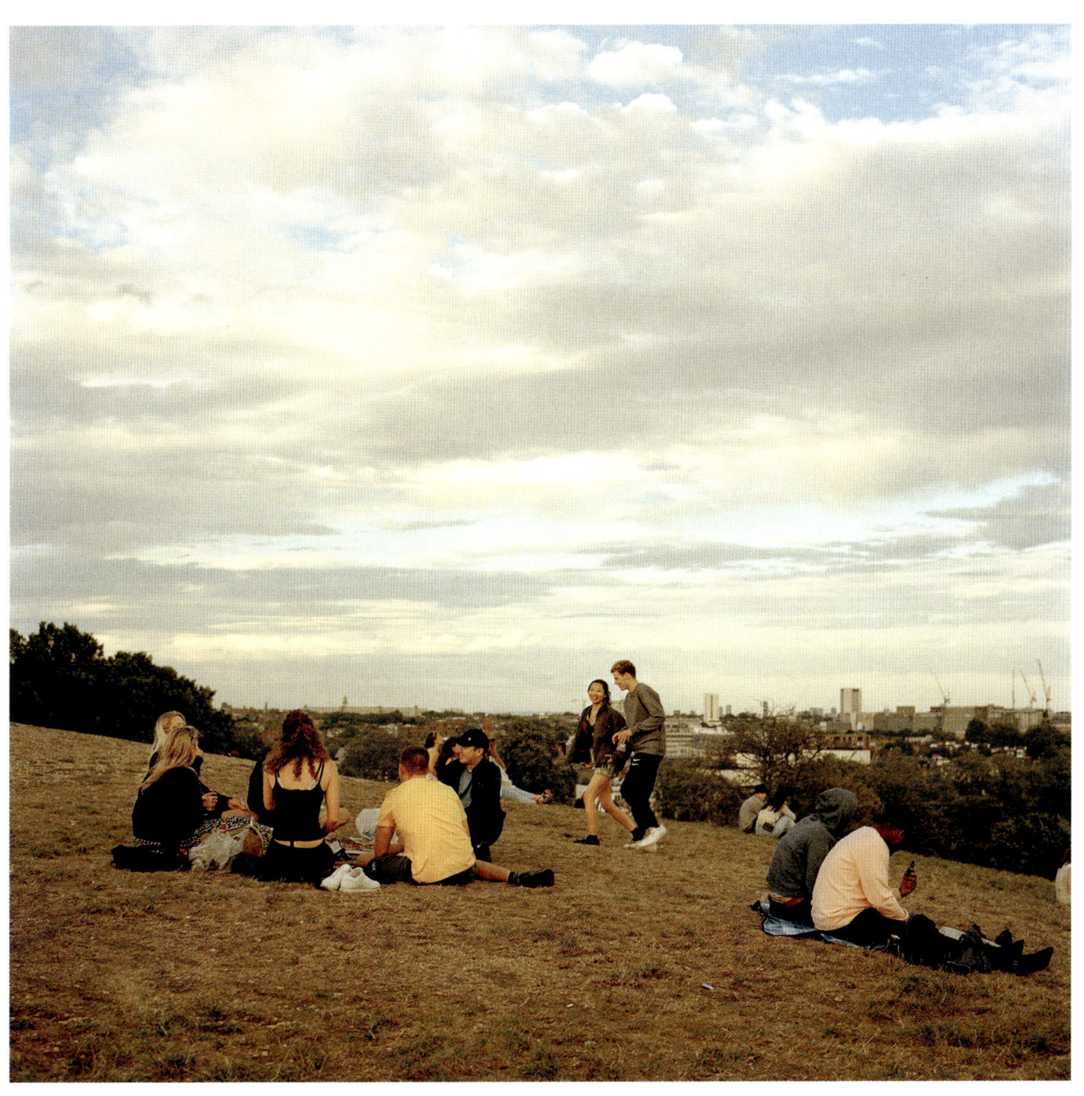

PRIMROSE HILL

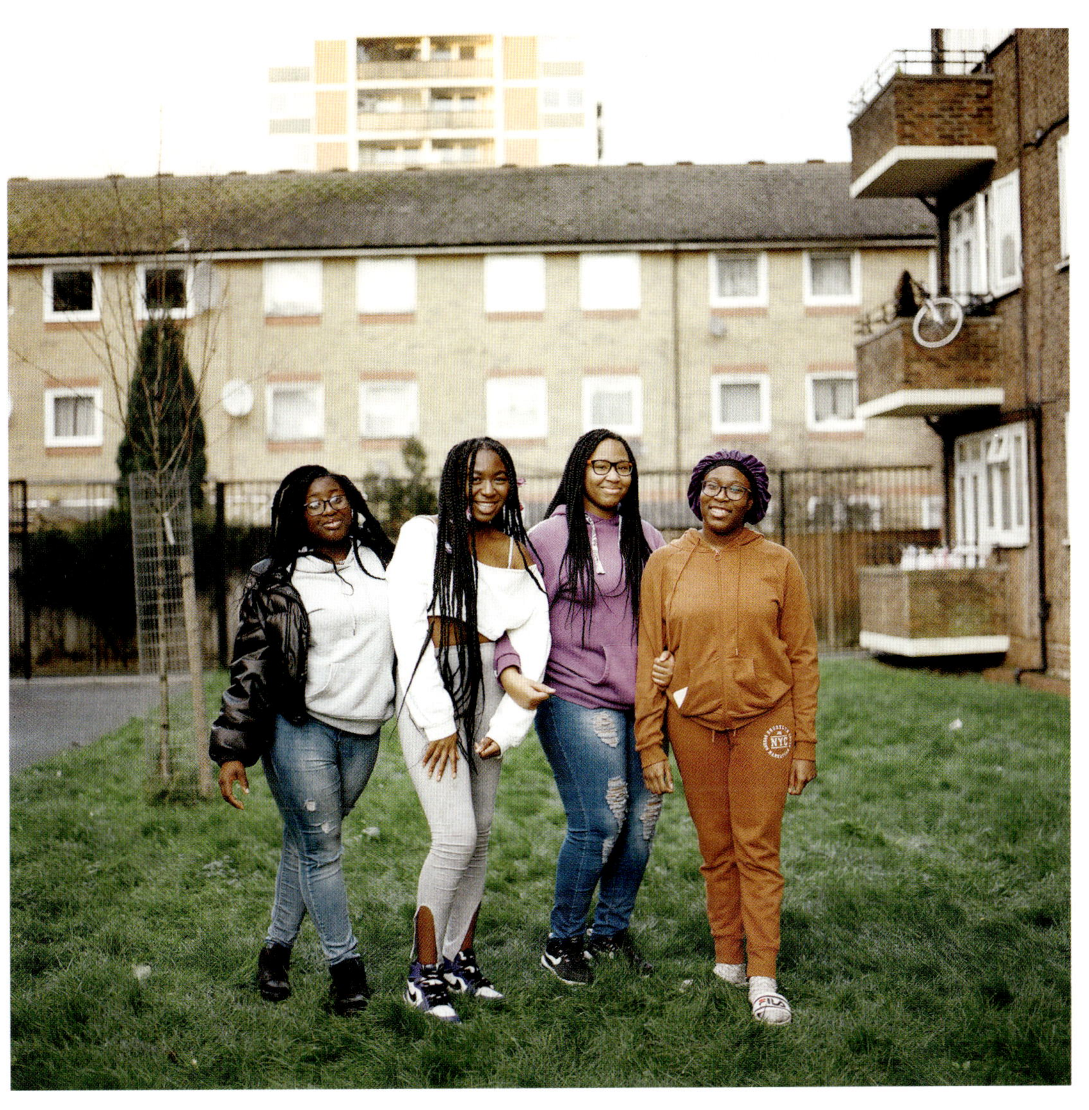

Pollyana, Yemi, Maya & Kely

MILTON GARDENS

'I love to walk here by myself listening to music and thinking.
It's a very isolated space that feels like it's hidden away so
I can pretend I'm not in London.'

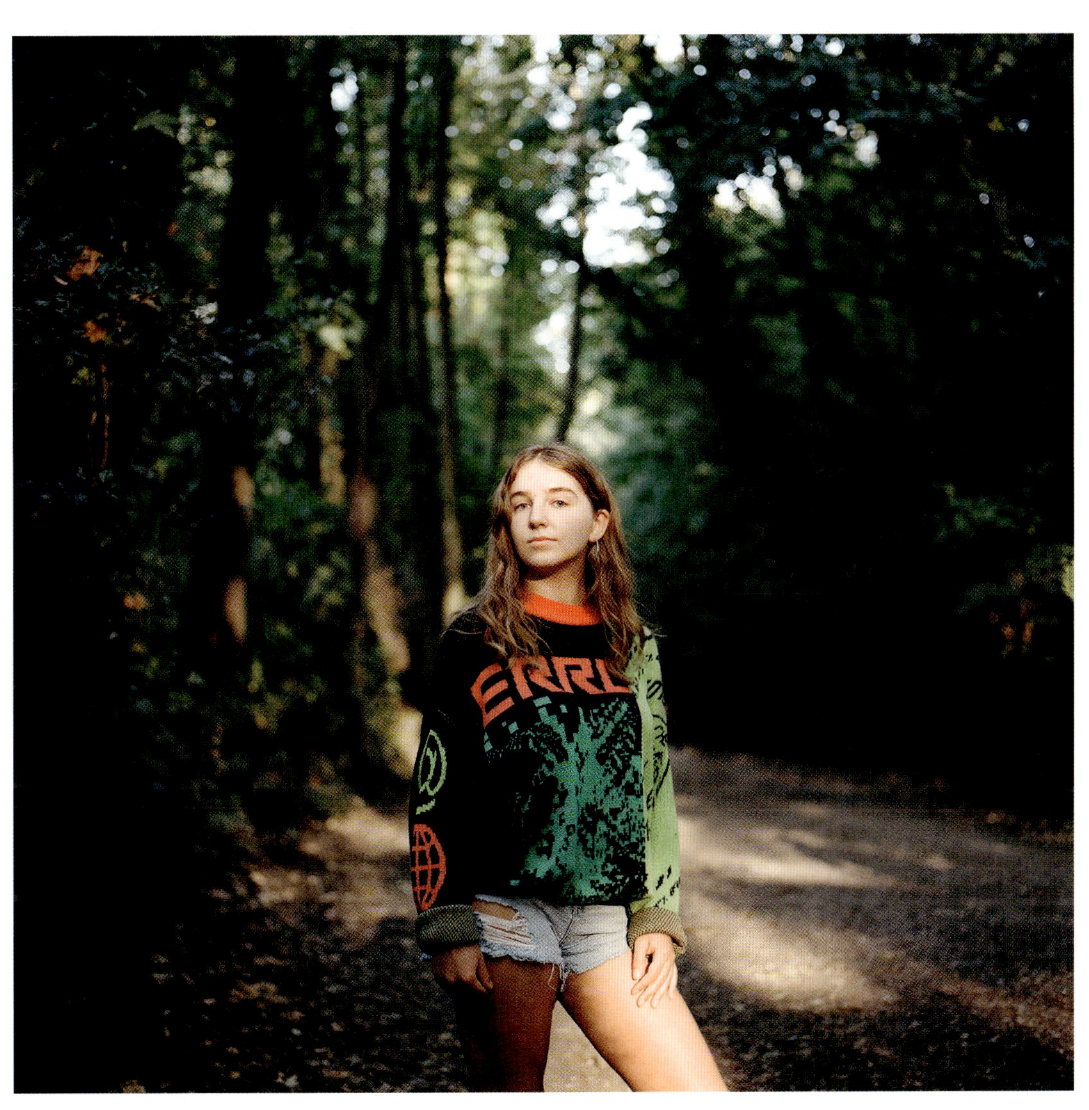

Kate

PARKLAND WALK

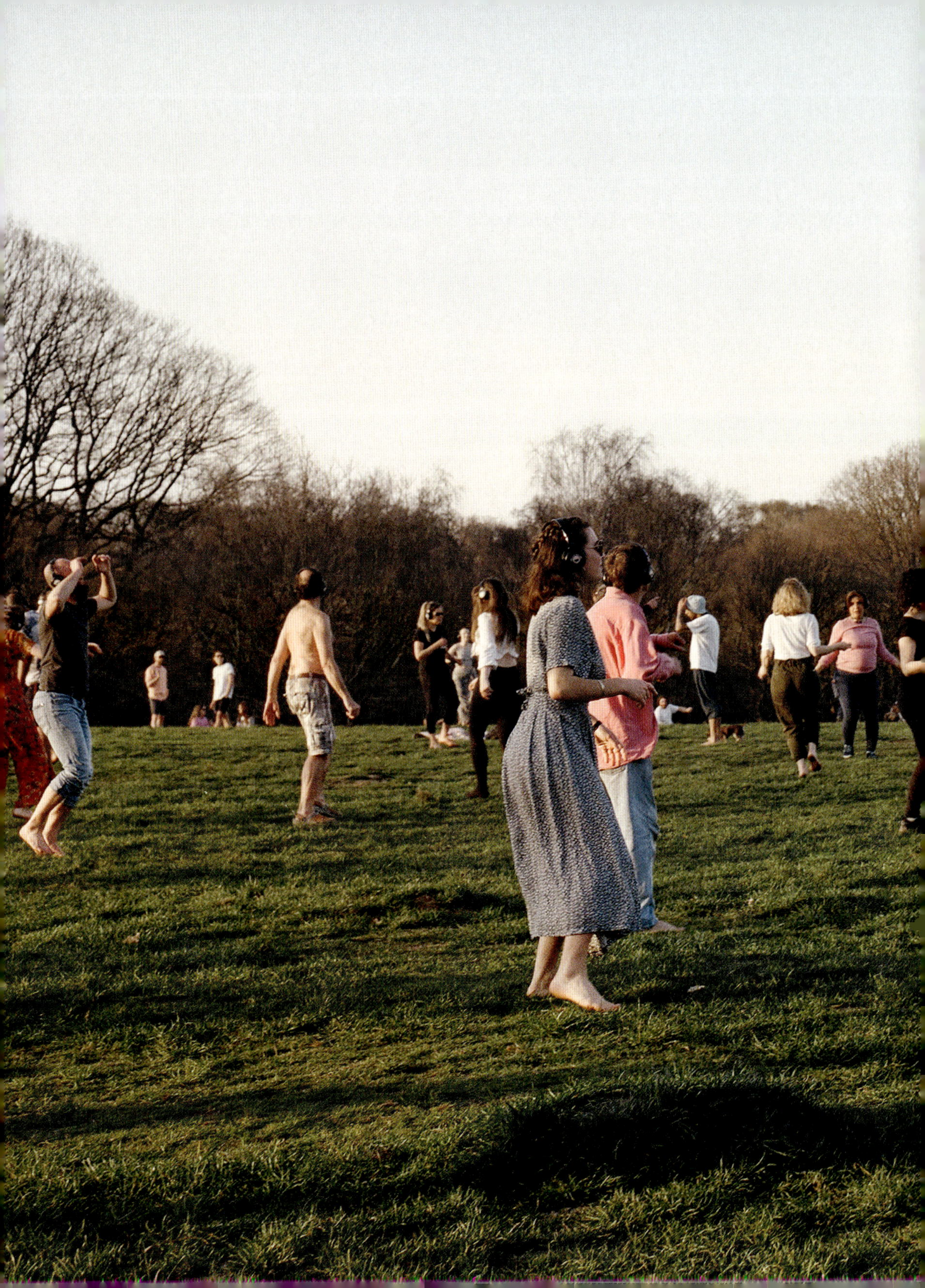

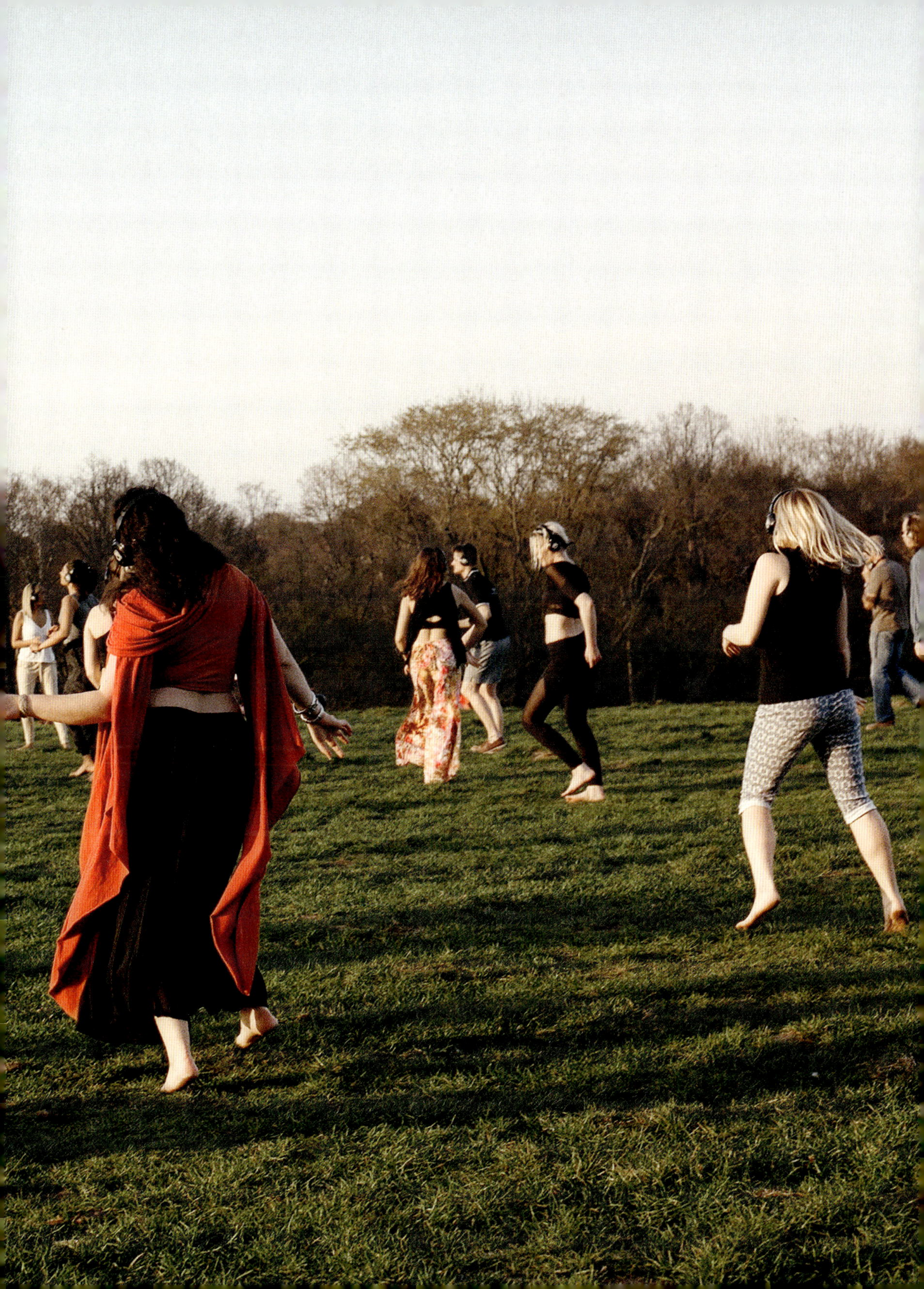

'I have special memories of taking my grandchildren to the
playground here – playing games and having ice cream at the café.'

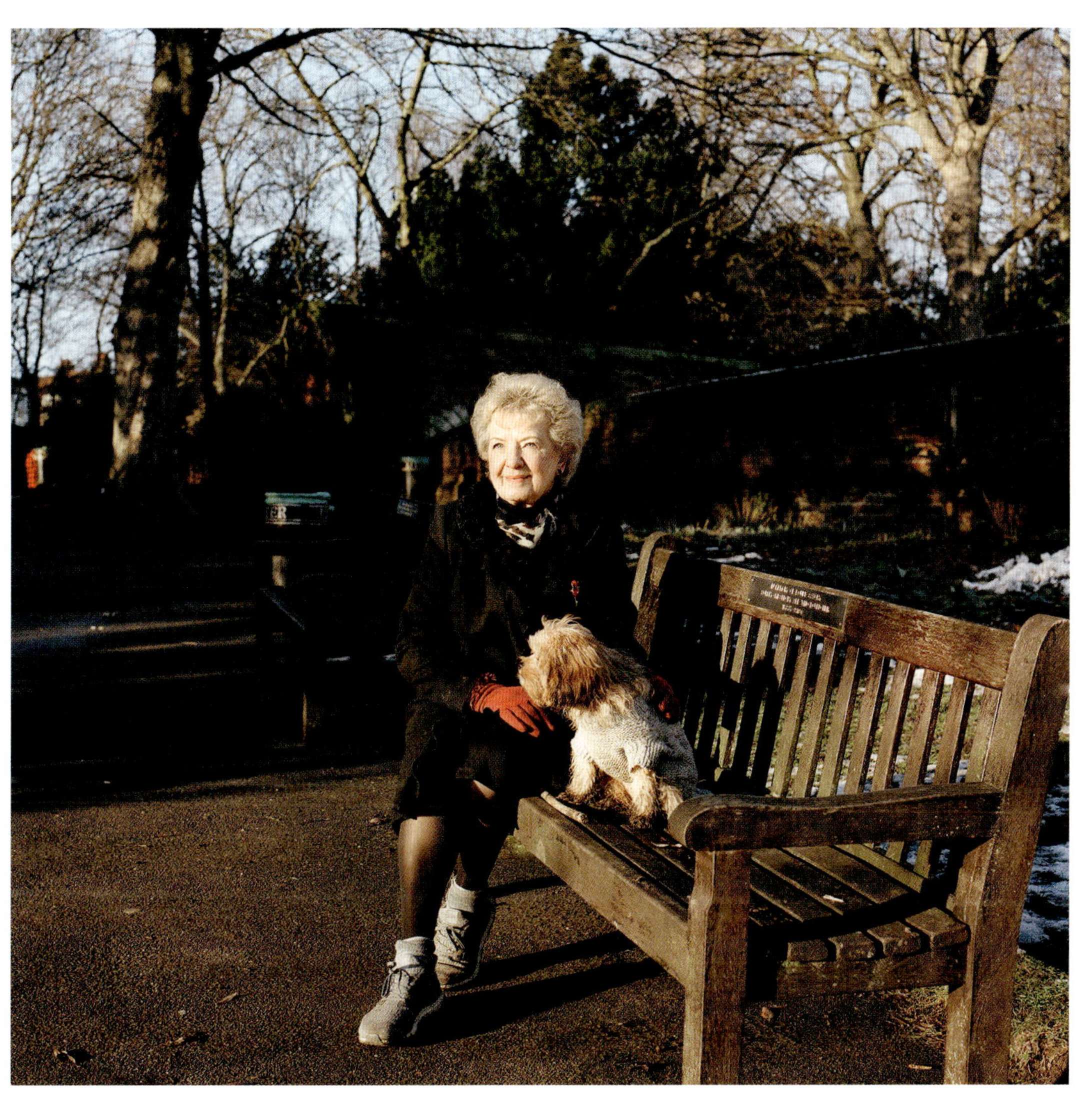

Brenda & Suki

WATERLOW PARK

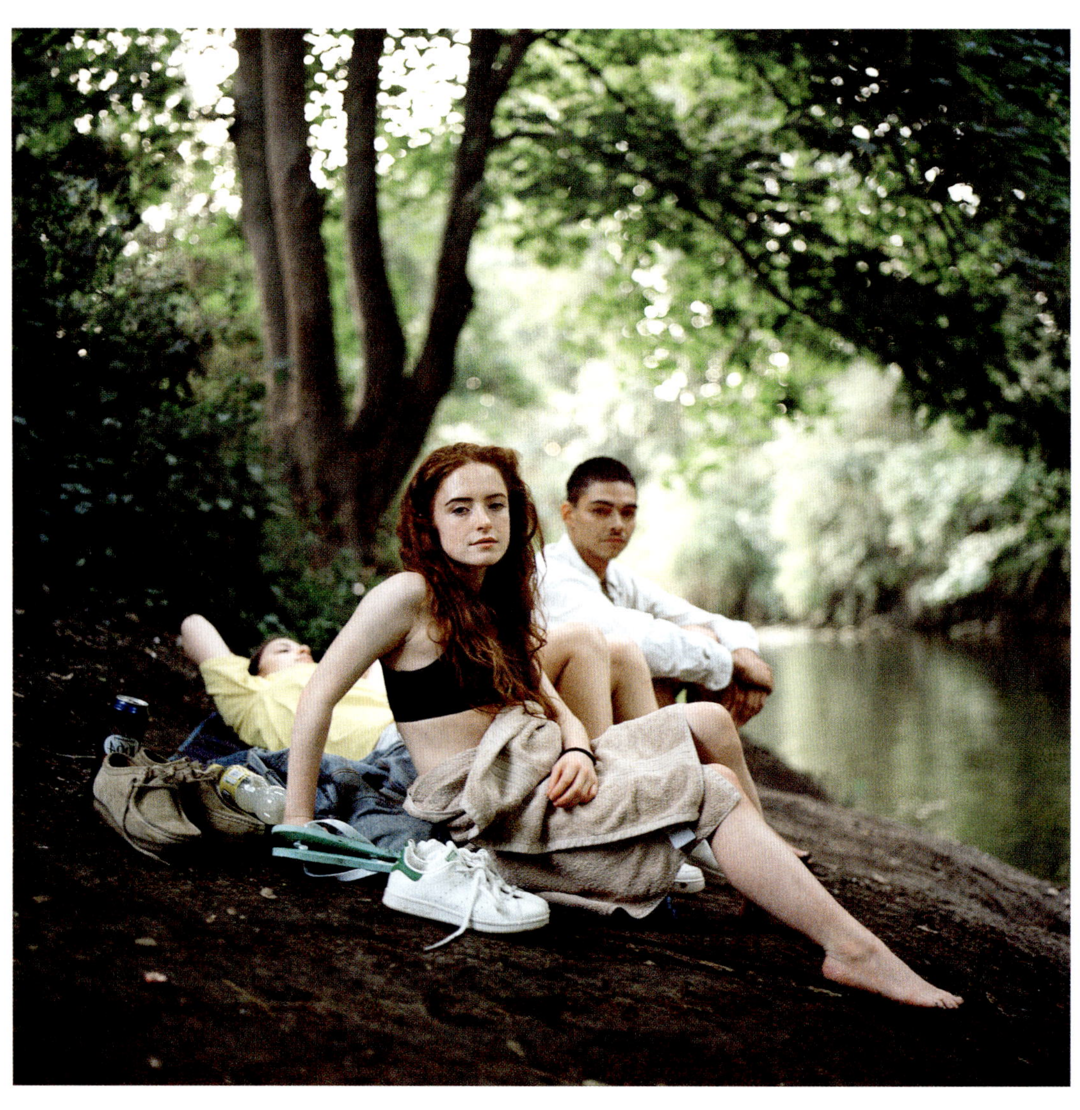

RIVER LEA

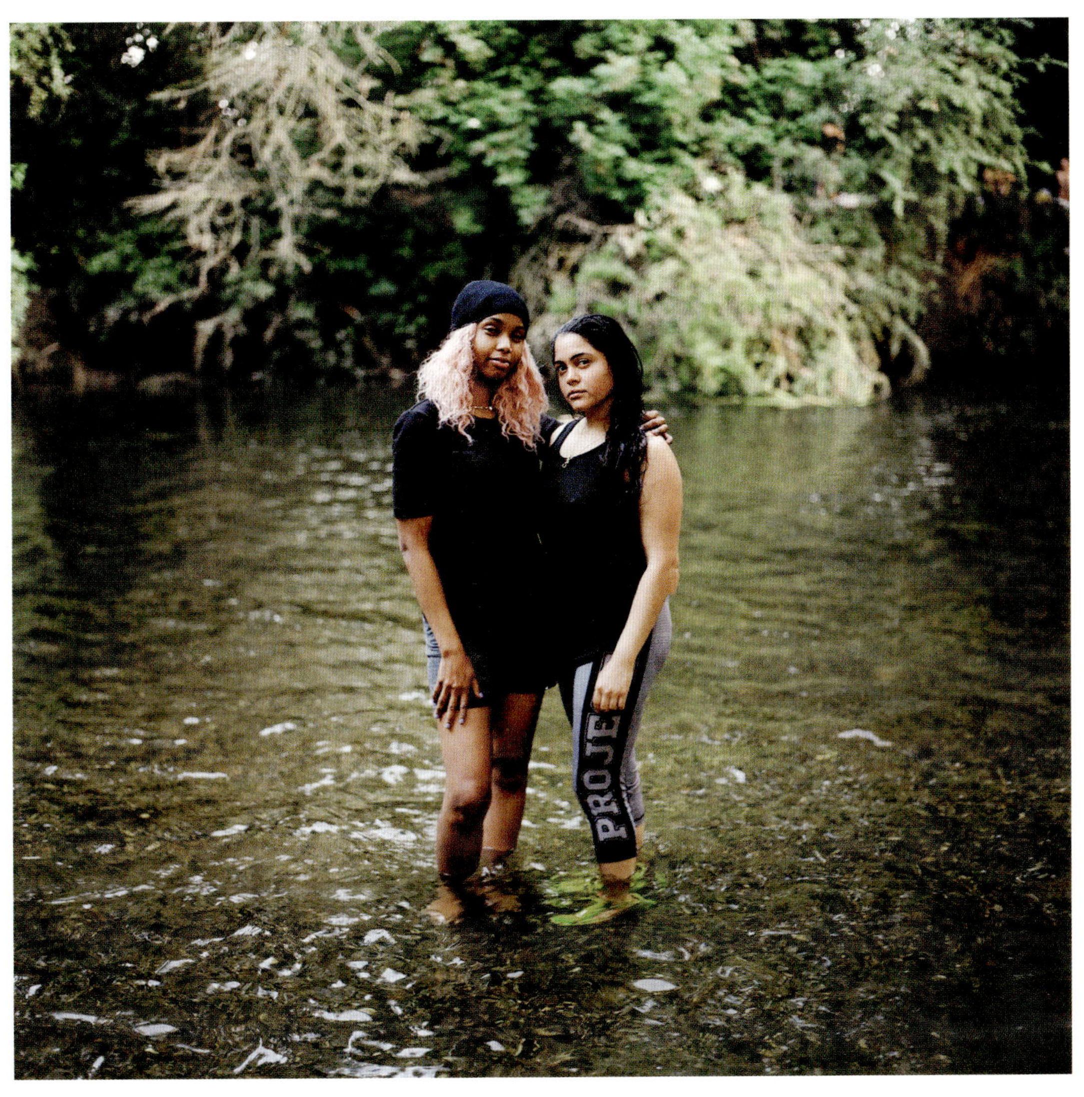

Anna & Diana

RIVER LEA

'Our apartment overlooks this end of Millfields Park,
so hopping the fence and walking through the trees is at least
a twice-daily occurrence. Saorlaith has grown up with the
resident jays, woodpeckers, parakeets, peregrines and kestrels;
she waves to each of them individually and alerts us
with her bird sign any time they pay the balcony feeders a visit.'

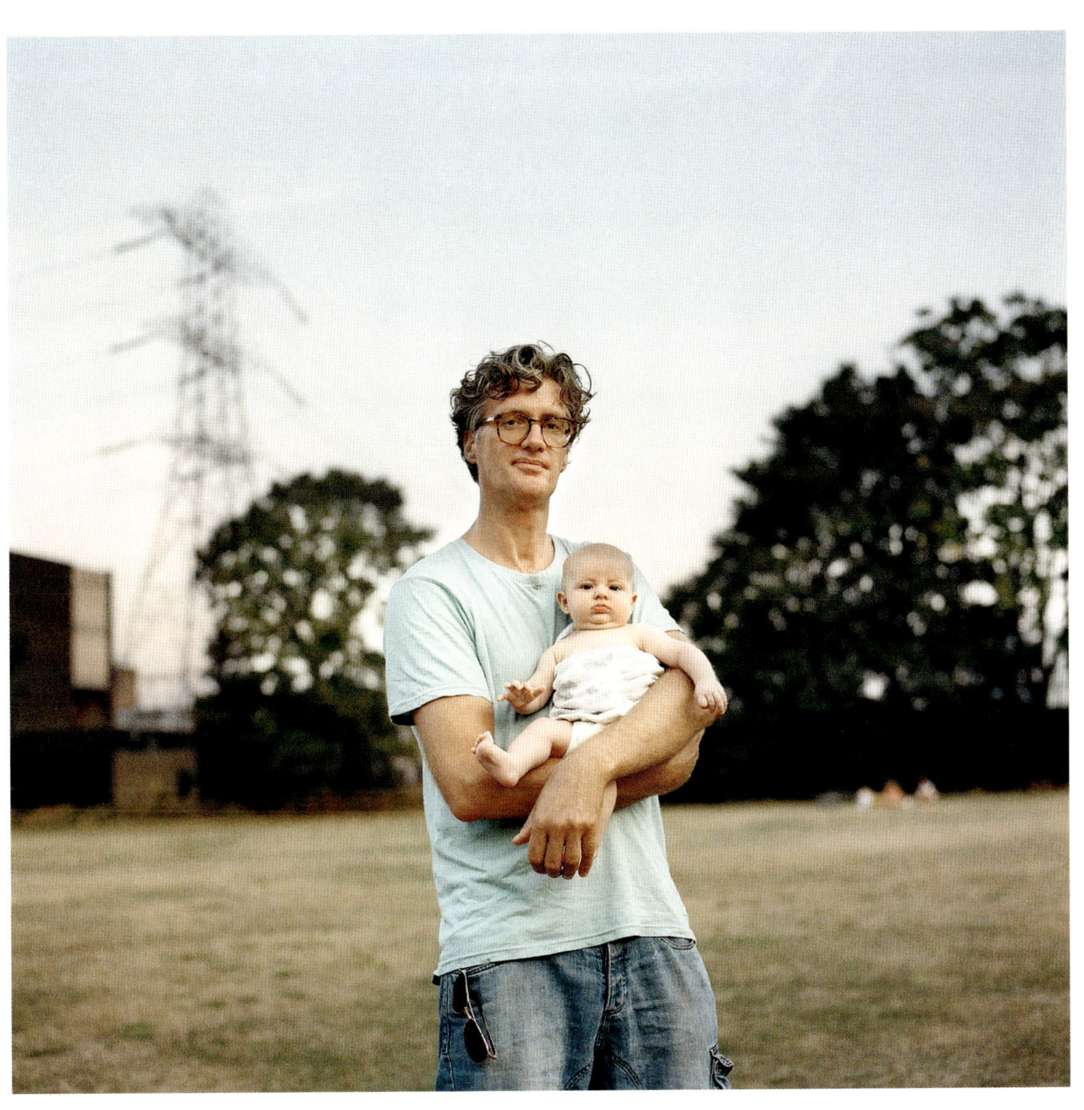

Brian & Saorlaith

MILLFIELDS PARK

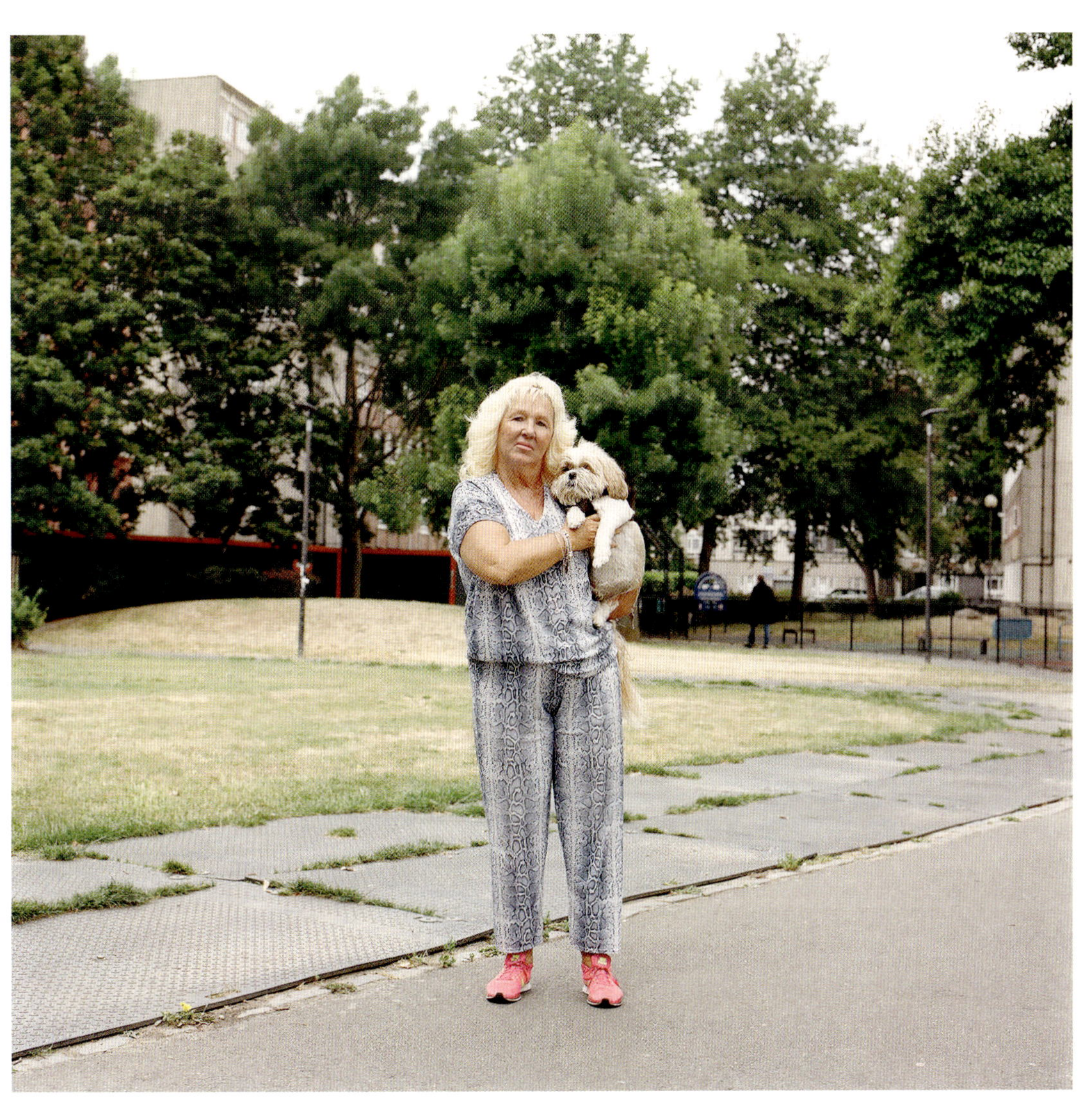

Sue & Fred

RAVENSCROFT PARK

'It's good to soak up the sun and feel the ground beneath your feet.
It reminds me to be present.'

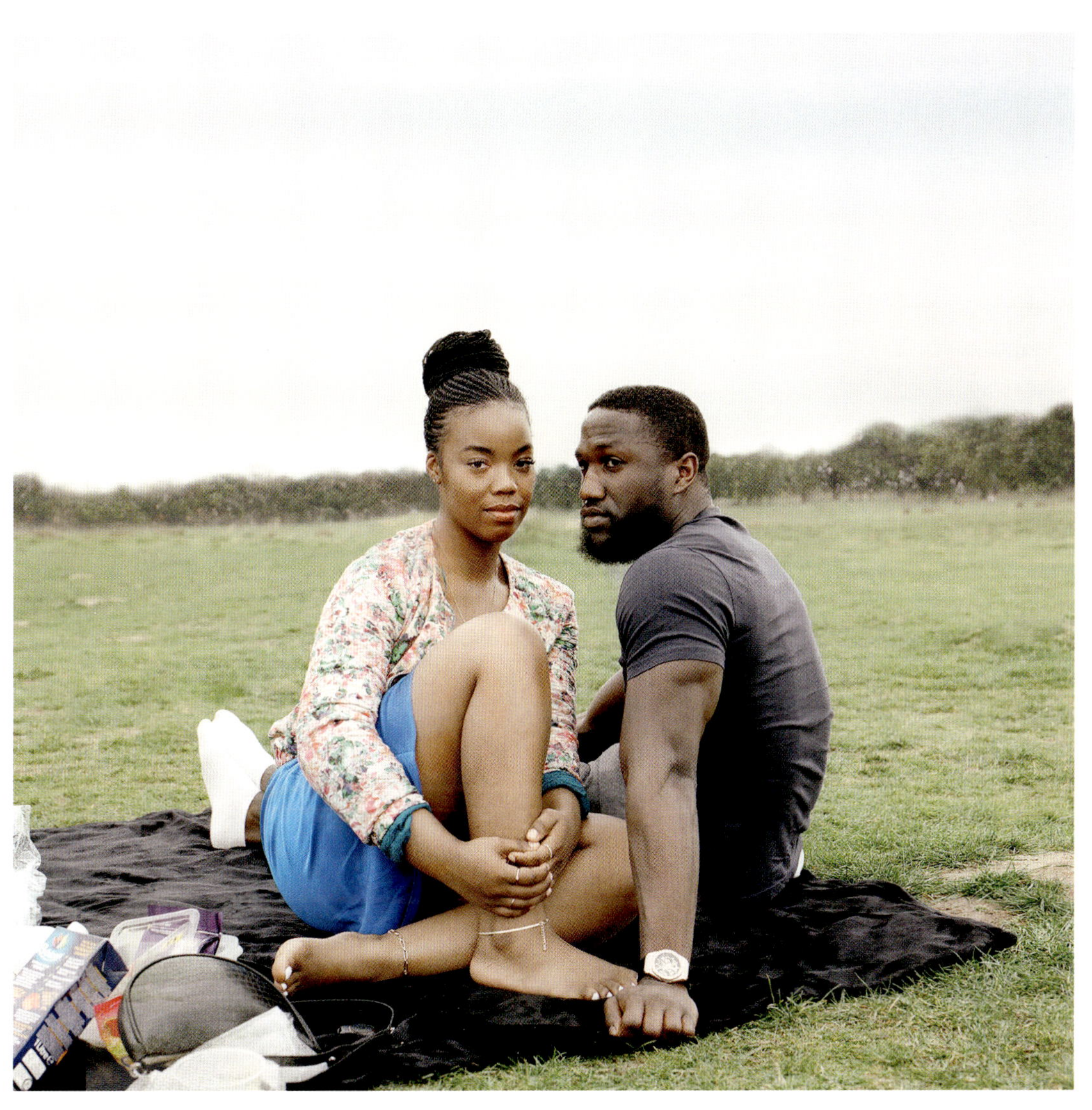

Rachael & Nick

RICHMOND PARK

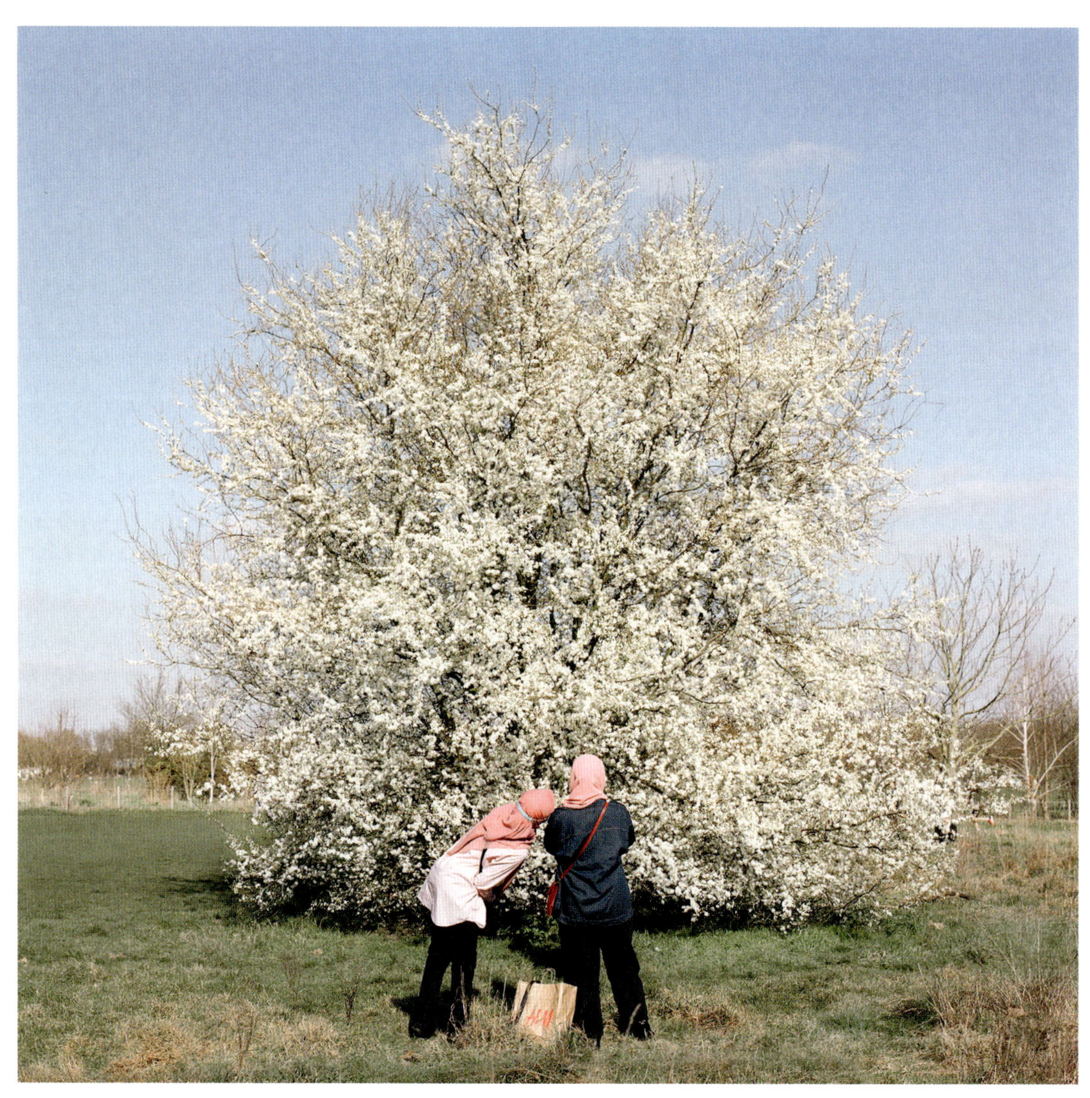

REGENT'S PARK

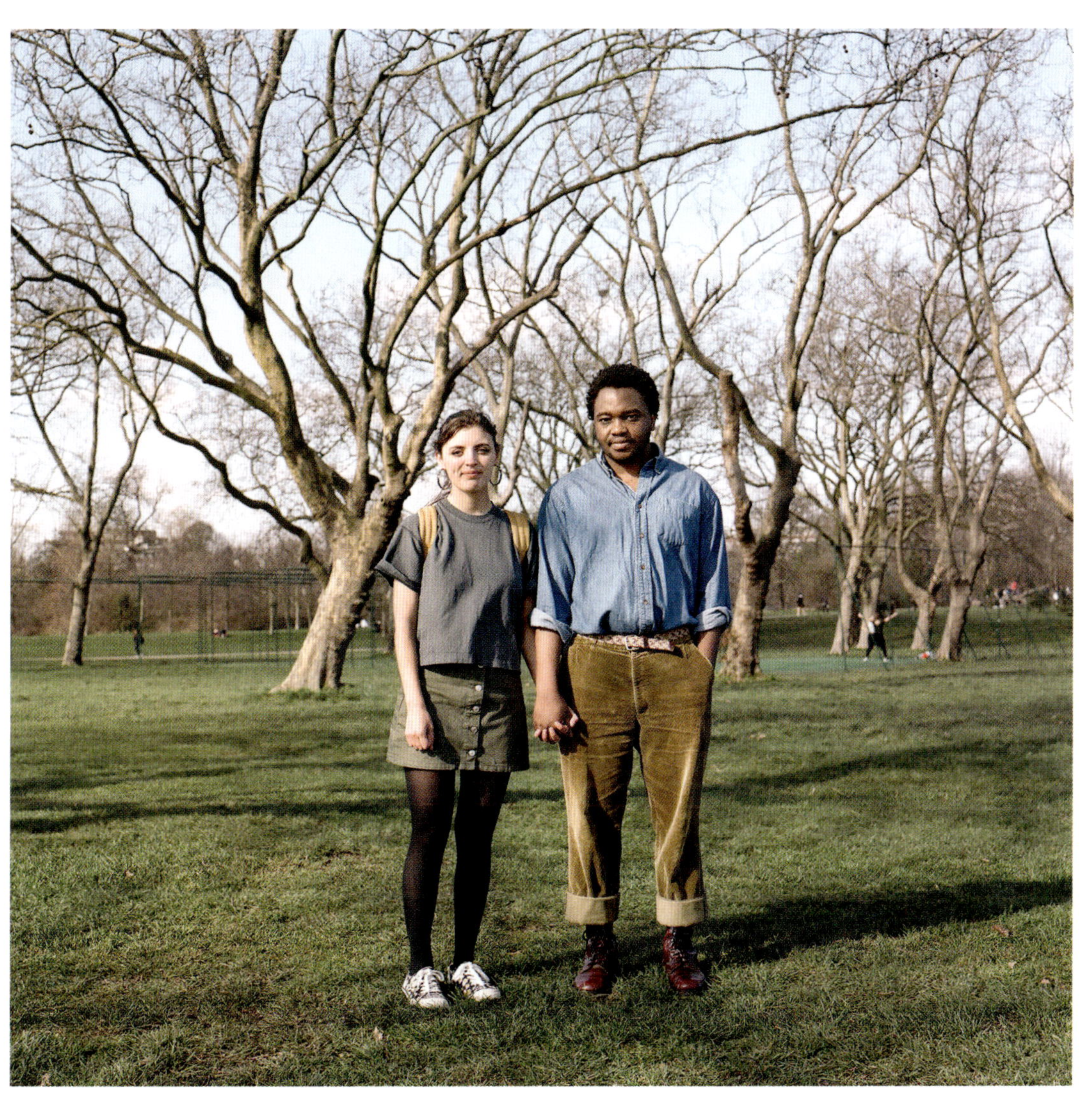

Eve & Arthur

REGENT'S PARK

'I've spent countless hours here sitting with friends,
a beer in hand and someone's speaker playing some tunes.
Hackney Downs was the first park I came to in London
where I sat down and said to myself, "Wow, I'm really living
in London. I'm here. I did it."'

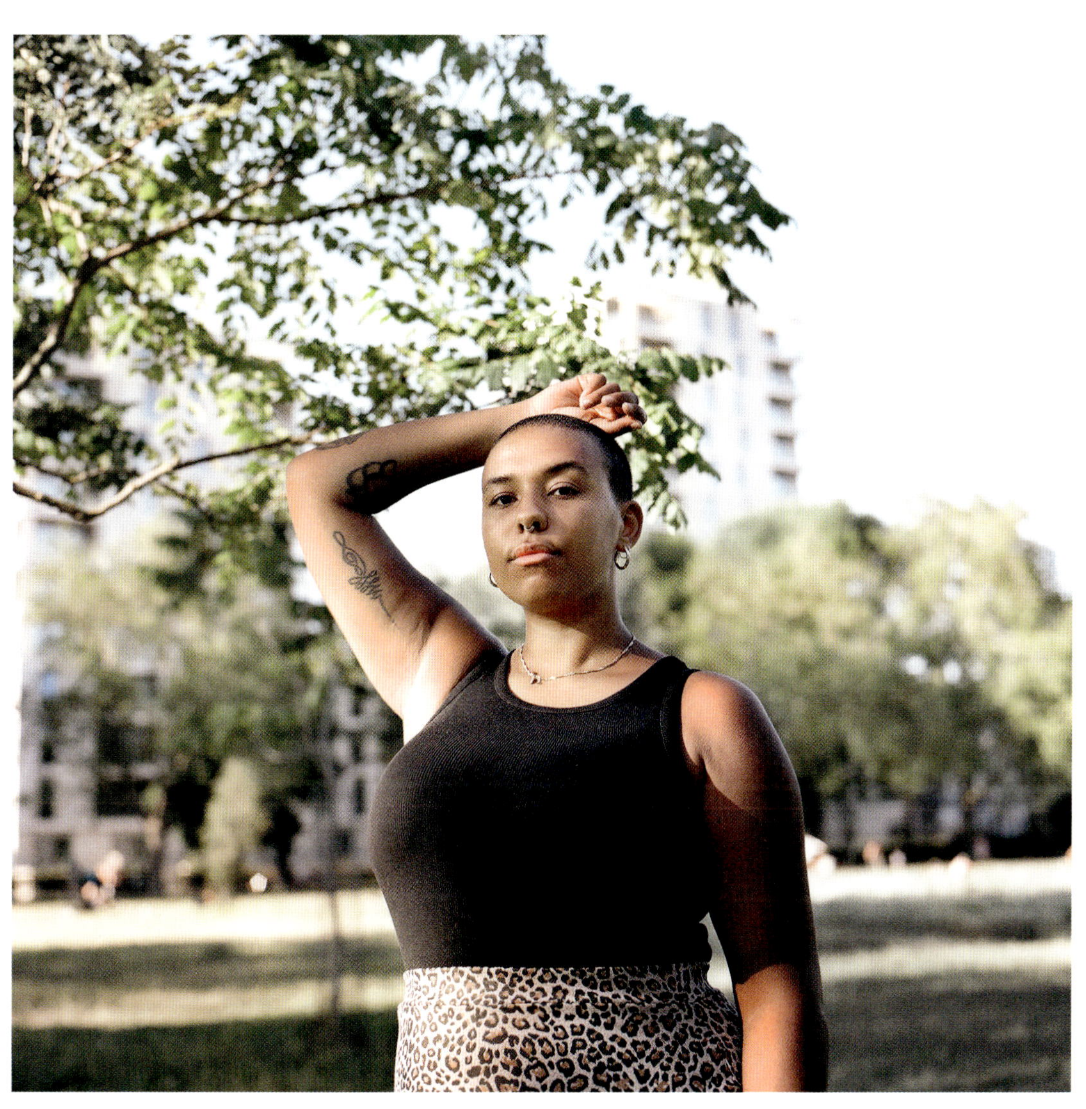

Claude

HACKNEY DOWNS

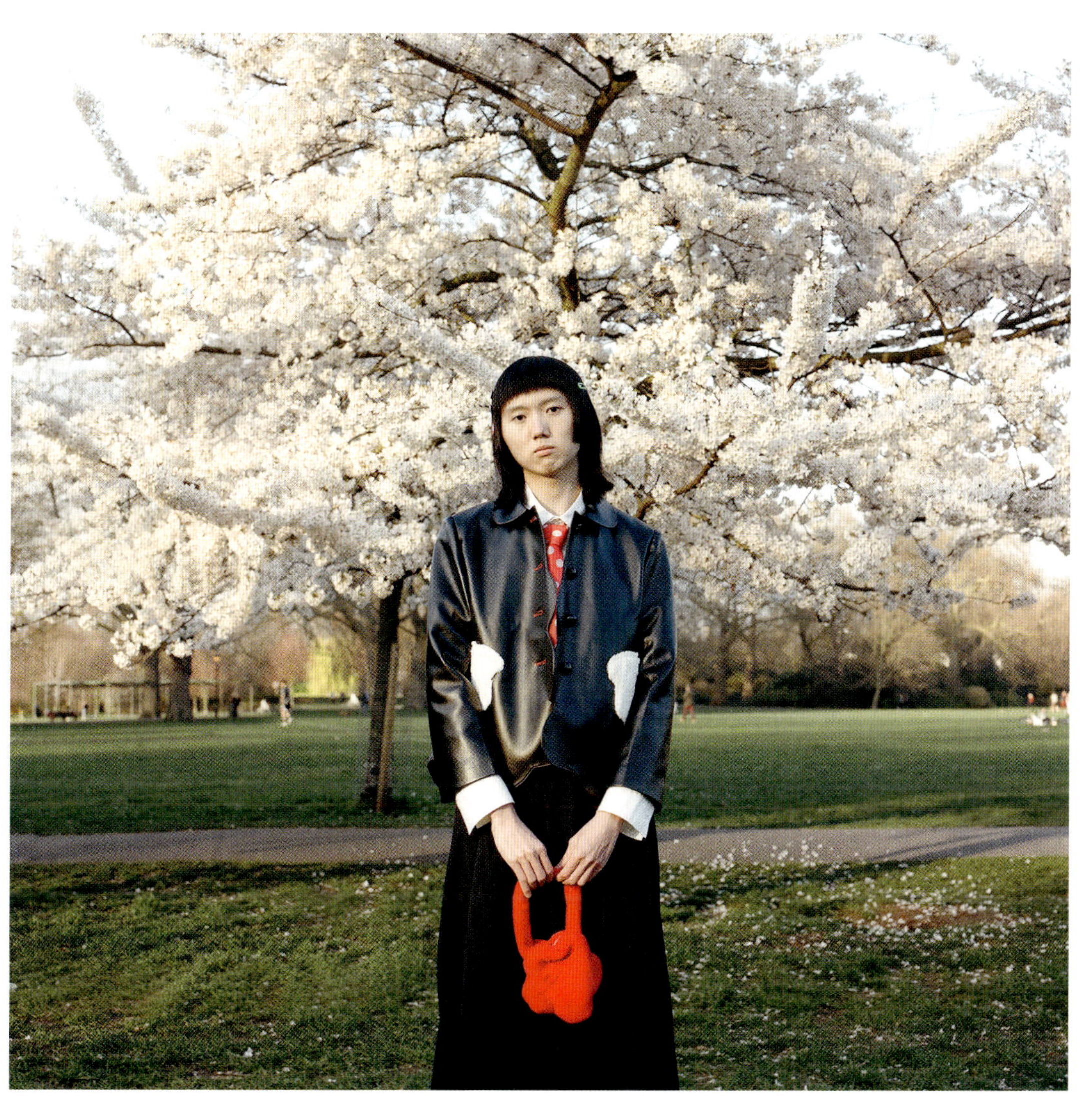

Dan

BATTERSEA PARK

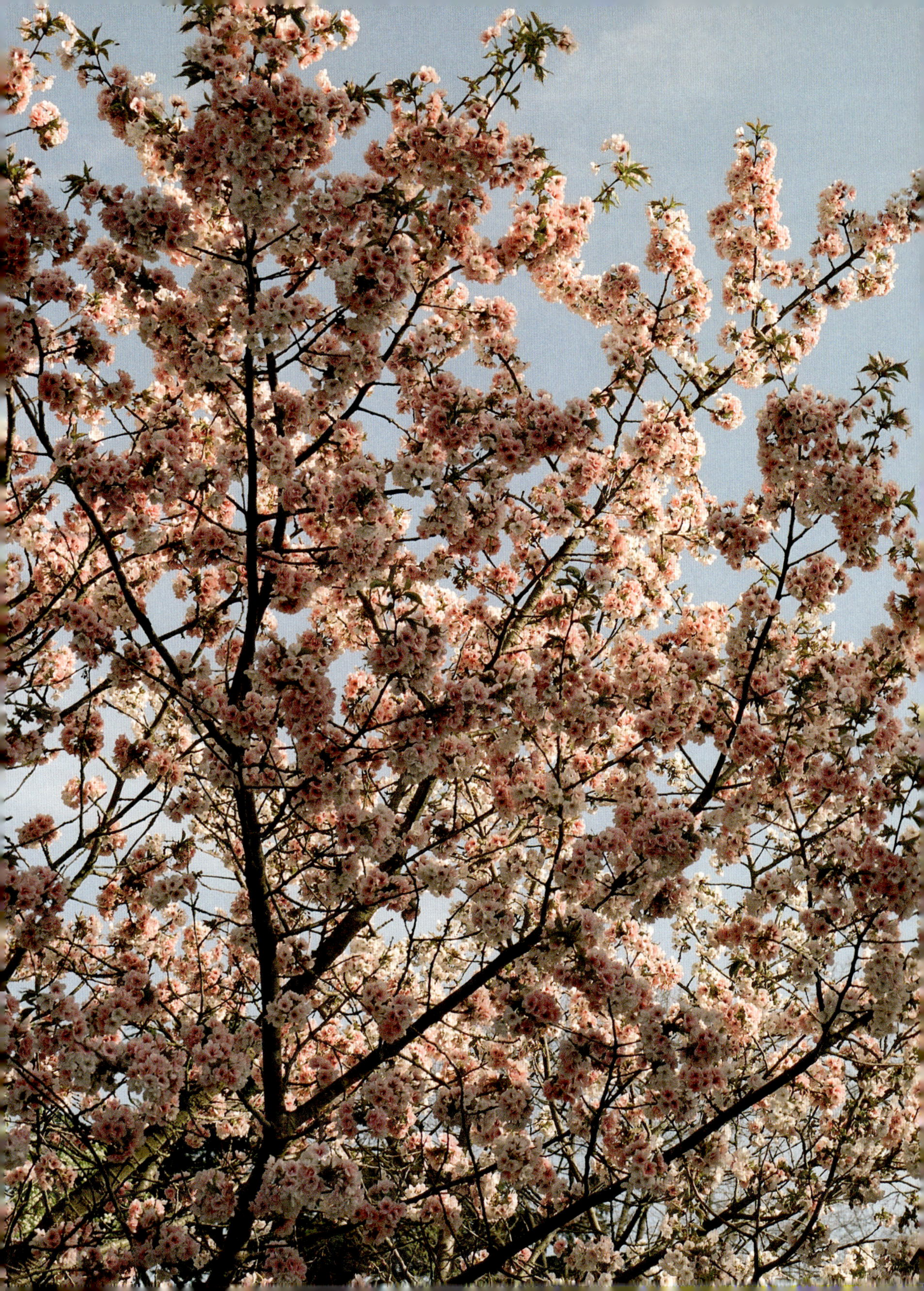

'My partner and I met as long-distance pen pals; I would
visit St James's Park to write to him. I vividly remember composing
a letter here, anxious and uncertain, but being bold enough to
take a chance on something that felt good. Now, three years later,
we visit this park when we can, and I often remember that
feeling – of being so fond of someone I only knew through words.'

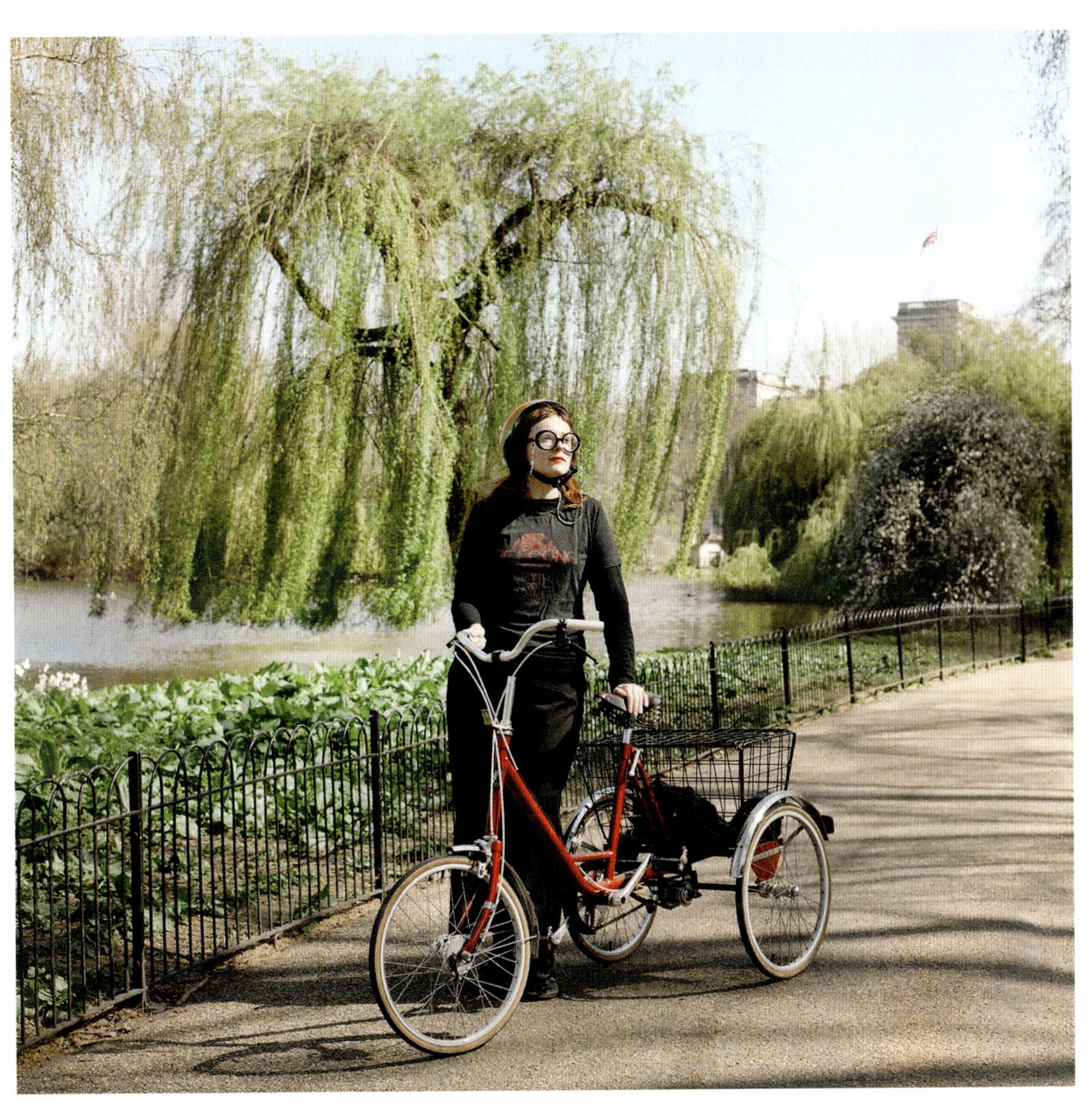

Lucille

ST JAMES'S PARK

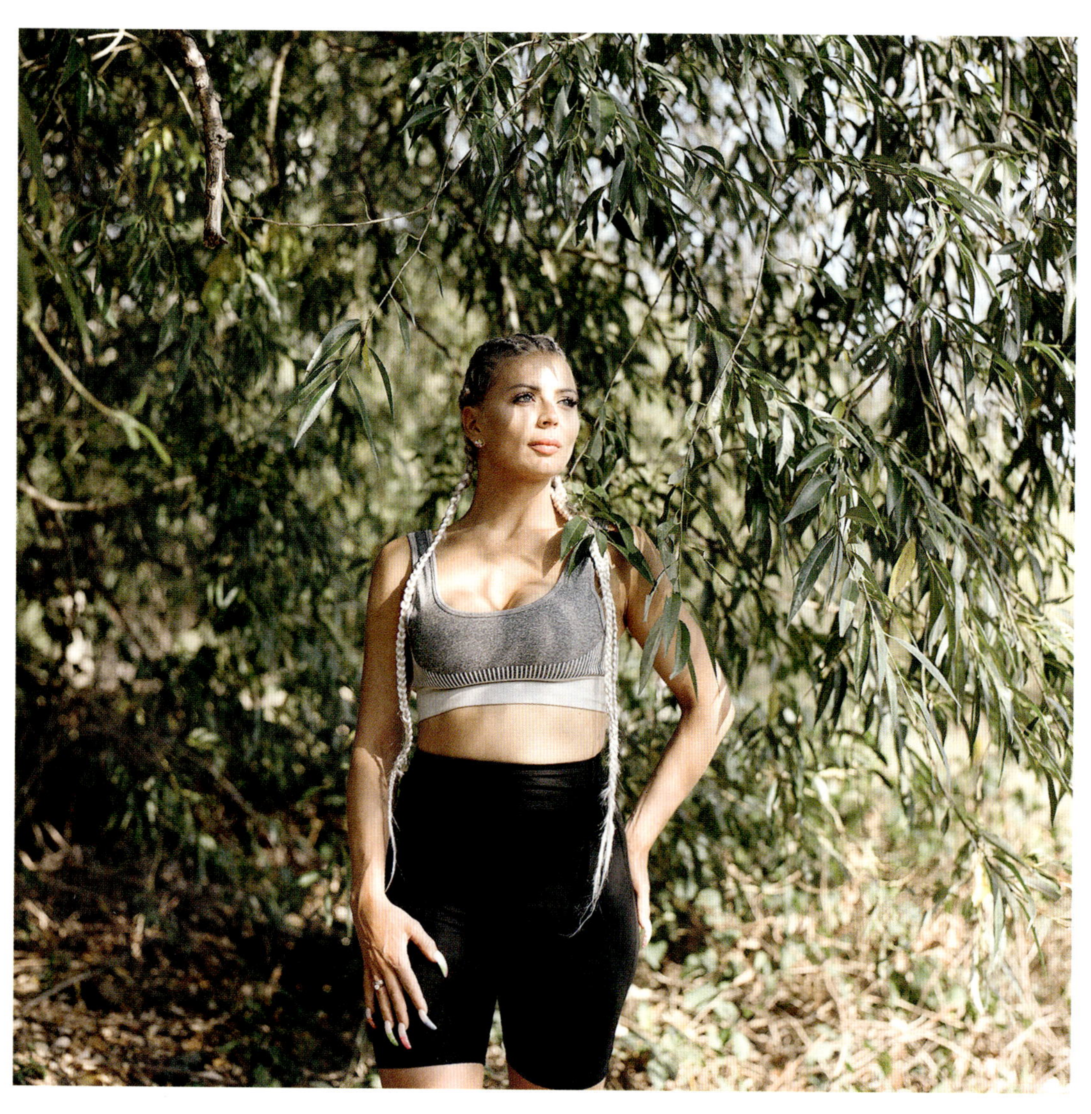

Natasha

GOLDERS HILL PARK

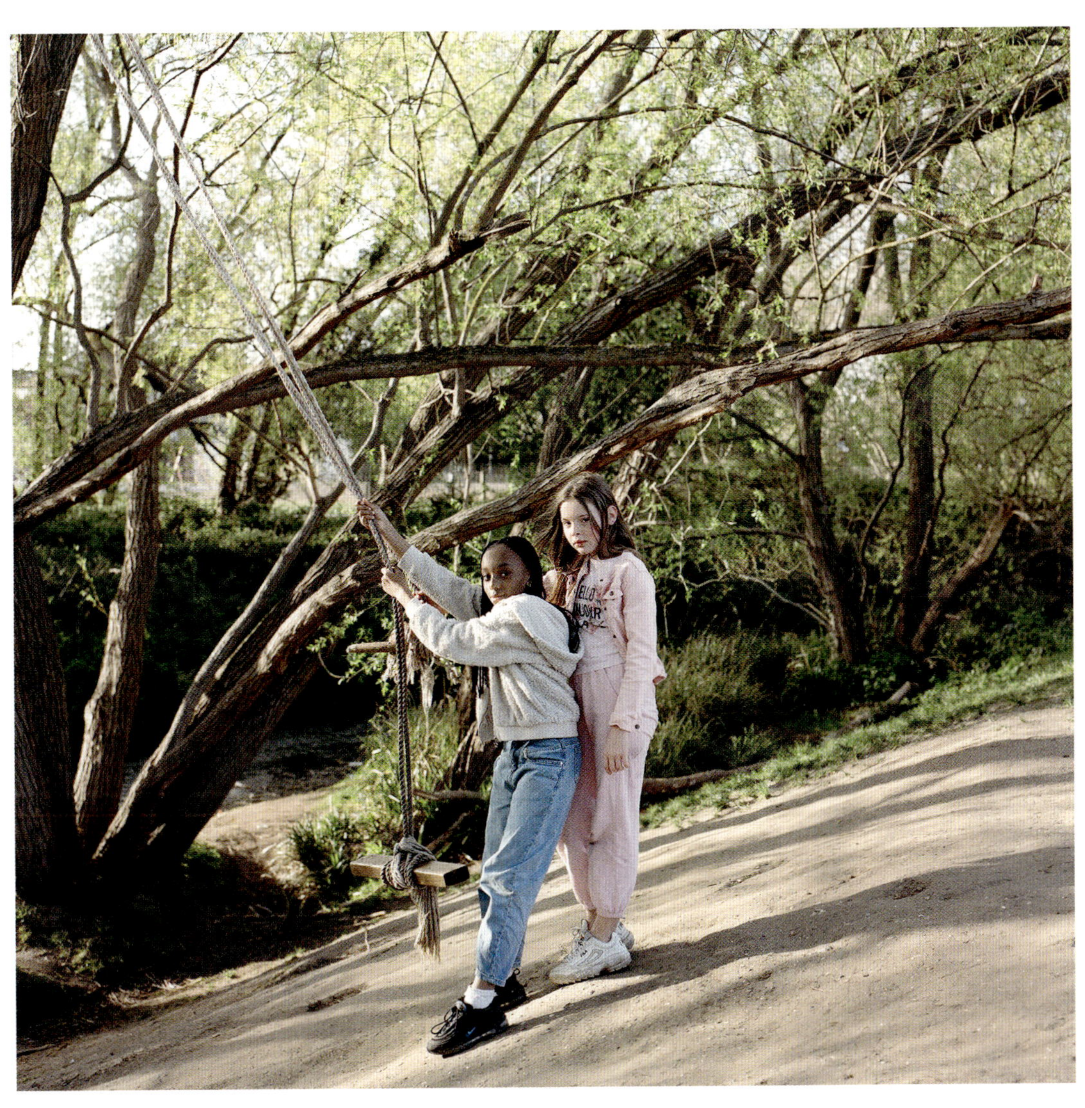

Lacey & Angel

WATERLINK WAY

'Out in nature, I don't feel that urgency to try and make
sense of my thoughts.'

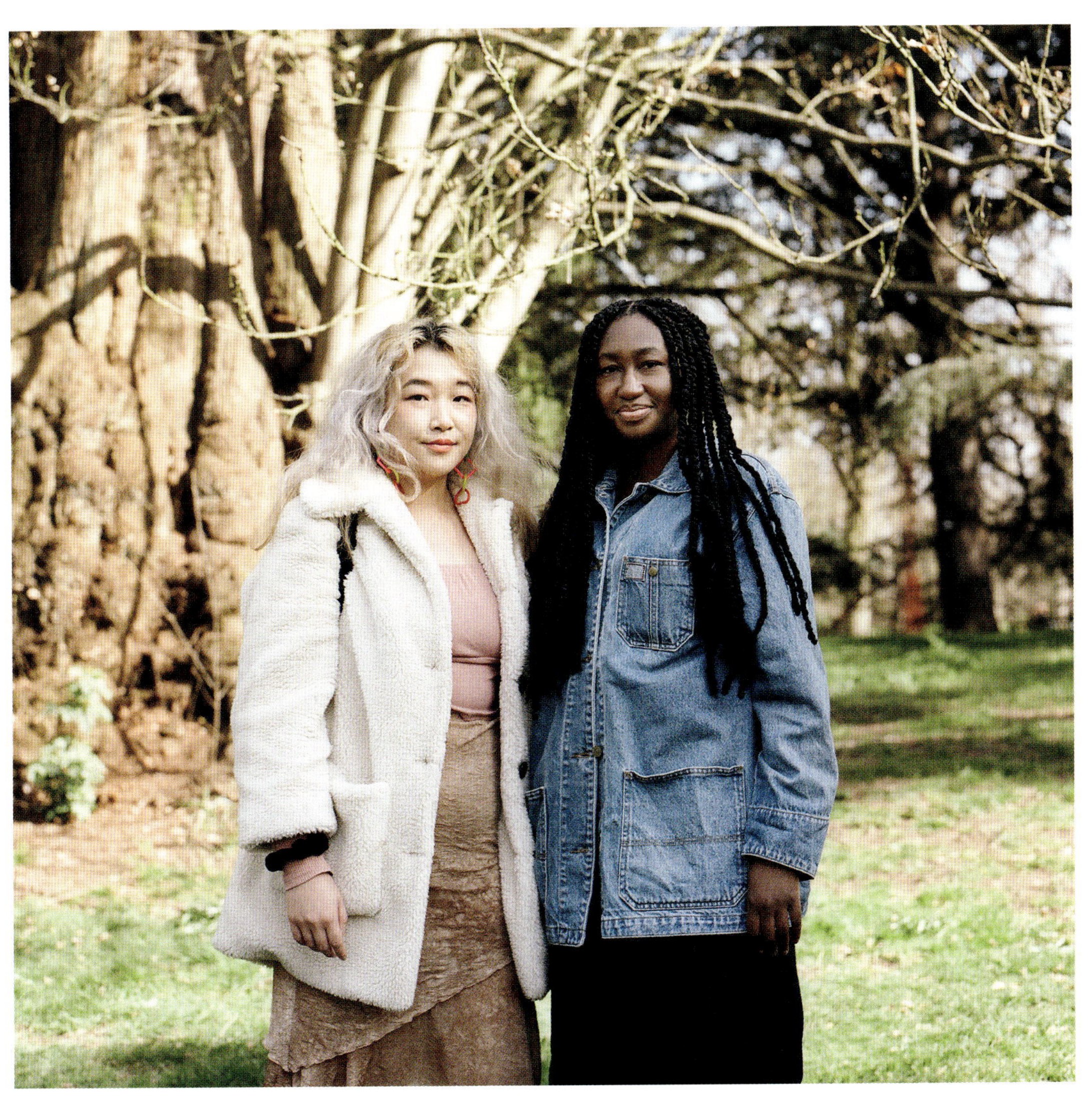

Ceecee & Ngadi

KEW GARDENS

'I grew up in London yet I'm still discovering parks and
woodland that I never knew existed. In the two years since my
daughter was born, we've been on countless adventures in
the wilderness, and all in the middle of a sprawling great city.'

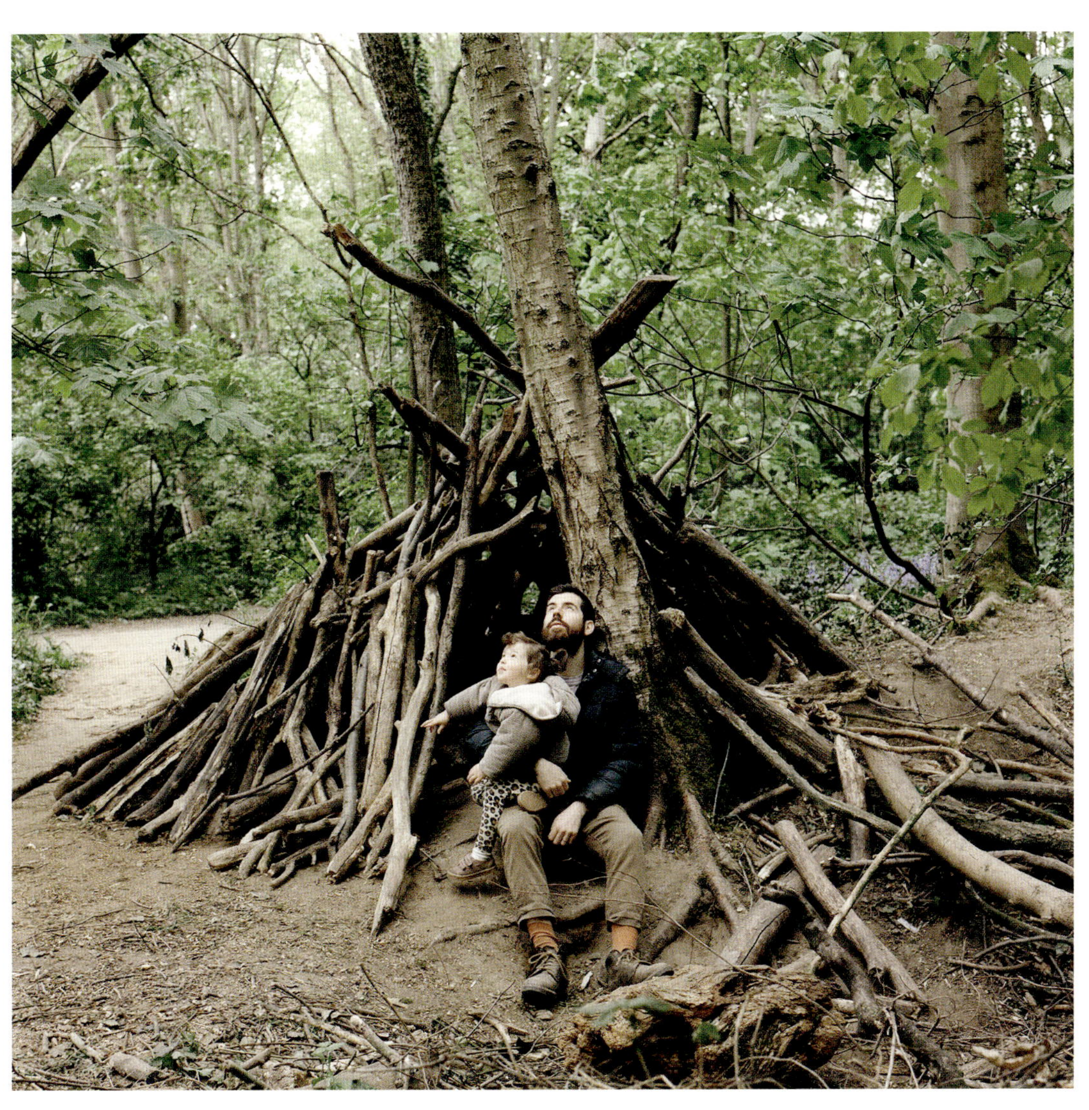

Maya & Ed

CHALET WOOD

Parklife
First Edition

First published in the United Kingdom in 2021 by Hoxton Mini Press
Copyright © Hoxton Mini Press 2021. All rights reserved.

All photographs © Sophia Spring
Introduction by David Nicholls
Design by Friederike Huber
Sequence by Friederike Huber and Sophia Spring
Copy-editing by Florence Filose
Design support by Daniele Roa
Production by Anna De Pascale

A CIP catalogue record for this book is available from the British Library.
ISBN 978-1-910566-99-2

The photographer would like to thank:
Everyone who made this book possible, in particular the team at Hoxton Mini Press –
Martin, Ann, Florence, Anna and Dani for their encouragement and patience. Fred for being so
generous with her time and entering into the spirit of true collaboration. David Nicholls for
elevating this series beyond my wildest imagination with his beautiful introduction. My parents,
Janie and Richard, for their unwavering support and love. My friends who've championed
this project along the way. Ed and Maya – the inspiration for everything I do. And most
importantly, all the people I photographed for this series (many of whom didn't make it into this
book). Without fail, every person I met reaffirmed my faith in human connection in some way.

This book is 100% carbon compensated according to ClimateCalc (climatecalc.eu).
Offset purchased from: Stand For Trees.
Printed and bound by: Livonia, Latvia.

For every book you buy from our website, we plant a tree:
www.hoxtonminipress.com

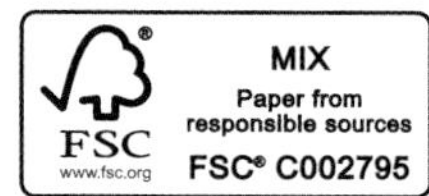